MW00616283

The Hidden History of New York:
A Guide for Black Folks

with special reference to the Metropolitan area

Third in a Series

DR. TINGBA APIDTA

A publication of:
The Reclamation Project
P.O. Box 191316
Boston, MA 02119
617-442-0563

Copyright © 1998 by Tingba Apidta.

All rights reserved. No part of this publication may be reproduced, stored in a retrieval system, or transmitted, in any form or by any means, electronic, mechanical, photocopying, recording, or otherwise, without the prior written permission of Tingba Apidta and the Reclamation Project. Printed in the United States of America.

Excelsior
(Ever Upward)

New York State Motto

The Hidden History of New York:
a guide for Black folks
by Tingba Apidta
The Reclamation Project Publishers
Includes bibliographical references and index.

Third in the Hidden Histories of America:
Guides for Black Folks series.

ISBN 1-892705-00-1

Manufactured in the United States of America

Table of Contents

Introduction

In 1991 workers in lower Manhattan uncovered 415 graves with as many as 20,000 of the forgotten Black builders of the "greatest city in the world." Discarded as rubbish in the ash can of New York history, the decayed bones of these tormented Black pioneers told a chilling tale. Stacked five deep they told of starvation deaths, chronic infections and unspeakable suffering. Muscles had been ripped from bone, necks had been broken and spines jammed into skulls—all injuries from lives cursed with carrying heavy loads. If they had not perished in infancy, they had lived just long enough to be worked to death.

Since the settlement of New Netherland (later named New York) Blacks have been well represented, though never welcomed, throughout the history of "The Big Apple." It is mythology to suggest that slavery and all its attendant atrocities did not reach the Empire State. The enslavement of Black Africans and Red Indians, as in the rest of the New World, was welcomed and even demanded by New York's European settlers. Consider this *Hidden History of New York*:

- Henry Hudson brutally murdered Indians after feasting and trading with them, beginning the Red Holocaust of New York.

- New York became the center of the slave trade and its bankers backed the growth of the plantation South.

- As many Americans were murdered in Manhattan in the anti-Black Draft Riots of 1863 as were killed in the War of 1812.

- At one time New York had a larger population of African slaves than did Maryland or Virginia.

This story of pure race hatred has masqueraded as a romantic chapter of New World settlement. It is every bit as genocidal as the accounts of the Nazi regime of a future century. New York's hidden history is here laid bare for all to see.

First Encounters
Red Holocaust: 1609-1674

When Henry Hudson pulled into New York harbor in 1609, he was not thinking of religious liberty or seeking relief from some despotic European ruler. He was little more than a trader under contract to a group of Dutch businessmen, seeking and acquiring wealth by whatever means necessary.[1] In later years such seaborne plunderers would be known as pirates. In this case, they were "explorers" who happened upon North America, seeking a shorter route to the riches of India. The local Red citizens would soon find out, in this "age of discovery," that European exploration and colonization actually meant the imposition of white supremacy and that they had all of two choices in the matter: cooperate or die.

Captain John Smith had employed that strategy with Pocahantas' people a few hundred miles to the south and encouraged his friend Hudson to try the same in the northern provinces. That Virginia experiment had resulted in the decimation of the Indians, the theft of their now blood-soaked land and the total submission of the Chesapeake Indians to English authority—a true Caucasian success story.[2]

But Hudson was not the first European to survey the New York region with eyes toward robbery. The Italian captain Giovanni da Verazzano entered what he called the "thickly inhabited" New York harbor in 1524. Sailing in the same year, right behind Verazzano, came Estevan Gomez, a Portuguese captain working for Spain.[3] Neither stayed long, leaving the prize to the Dutch marauder Henry Hudson decades hence.

Native Hospitality, Hudson's Brutality

Henry Hudson was the one who initiated exploration of the land that would become the greatest city of all time. The Indians welcomed and feasted with Hudson's pale entourage, even assisting them to repair the ship's damaged mast. In his diary, Hudson acknowledged his warm reception:

> On our coming...mats were spread out to sit upon, and immediately some food was spread served in well-made red wooden bowls; two men were also despatched at once with bows and arrows in quest of game....[4]

As in nearly all accounts of the early European explorers, the Native people were hospitable to the European to a fault. The Canarsie chief showered Hudson with gifts and restocked his ship's holds with beans, wheat, oysters and fish. Some crew members stayed as guests to establish trade while awaiting the ship's return voyage from Europe. They were even offered female companionship from within the tribe.[5]

Despite the peaceful offerings and the great bounty bestowed upon Hudson and his crew, Hudson responded with customary viciousness. After one of the many feasts provided for the Europeans by the local chief, one curious brave sought to examine some European clothing. He was shot in the chest and killed by one of the crew. The frightened Indians fled in their canoes, while some jumped into the water. When a struggling brave reached to hold on to the boat, Hudson's cook "seized a sword and cut off one of his hands and [the Indian] was drowned." Later, Hudson attempted to kidnap two young Red men, who escaped and called their people to retaliate. When they shot their arrows at Hudson's ship, six muskets replied, killing two or three of them. The ensuing battle left several more Indians dead.[6]

The violence associated with Indian encounters could not have been initiated by the kindly natives. Hudson himself dispels that myth:

> The natives are a very good people, for when they saw I would not remain, they supposed that I was afraid of their bows, and taking their arrows, they broke them in pieces, and threw them into the fire.[7]

The Europeans further patrolled the inland waterway, feigning brotherhood while fishing and trading. Upon encountering another peaceful Indian village, Hudson's crew drove them from their dwellings and stole their belongings—"as they would have done of us," they reasoned. This may have been one of the first New World applications of the oft-used "pre-emptive strike." The startled Red citizens countered with an arrow to the throat of one of the crewmen. Several of the Indians were murdered at the hands of Hudson's men and two were captured and dressed up in red coats and paraded around the ship for their amusement. "The practice of kidnapping natives in those days was almost universal," author Llewelyn Powys assures us. Indeed, Verazzano, Gomez, Columbus and Vespucci, among others, had engaged in the common European practice of kidnapping the indigenous peoples—the European's first New World export.[8]

Such was the nature of the first encounter of Red and white in earliest New York. Hudson would return to his employers, reporting success and opportunity. The New York Indians would warily anticipate the second European wave.

Settlement, Slaughter and Slavery

How, indeed, could he have foretold...that the traders, who followed in his wake, and who were to barter for furs behind well-built stockades, would, in their turn, be succeeded by well-established settlers, who would gradually exterminate his people, lay low his mighty forests, and construct upon the wild earth, township and citadel, divorced entirely from the manner of living he knew and loved?[9]

Though permission from the original landowners was neither sought nor granted, New Netherland was formally created in June of 1623 with thirty families and a shipload of 103 horses and cattle. The Dutch West India Company, a private wealth-development firm of Holland, established the area's first European settlement on the site of present-day

Albany. Soon, the Company's director Peter Minuit settled himself on Nut (or Governor's) Island, and from there "purchased" the 22,000-acre island occupied by the Manhattes, for twenty-four dollars worth of trinkets. This was the beginning of the settlement of New York in 1626 and the beginning of the end for the Red man.[10]

The carnage of the European onslaught was only amplified as the settlement grew. The instructions from the Company's directors back in Holland established ground rules for their land-snatching policies. Land should be acquired fairly, they said, "lest we call down the wrath of God upon our unrighteous beginnings."[11] The advice was thoroughly ignored.

Indian Civilization: Fruit of 10,000 Years

The European had set his destructive impulses on more than a few "huts" and "savages." His victims were by no means "uncivilized" and therefore worthy of their own demise, as the Euro-historians like to recall them. Early white accounts confirm that the culture of the Indians was impressive. They were skilled healers, having developed medicinal remedies to cure many ailments. They could cure the white man's venereal infections so readily, that "many an Italian master who saw it would be ashamed of his profession." Their health regime was superior. According to another account, "Most of the diseases incident to females of the present day were unknown to them." Agriculturally, they had developed at least twenty different varieties of corn and farmed the much-coveted maple sugar. With little overt legal structure, criminality among them, as one Dutch authority remarked, "was of remarkably small consequence." Their superior skills at fur trapping, in fact, financed the colony and made wealthy not a few European furriers.[12]

The Iroquoian Confederacy, or Six Nations, occupied the upstate New York area and spoke for the Indians there. The Confederacy was organized in 1570 for the mutual safety of the member nations. The governmental structure, particularly the level of participation of the women, was extraordinary by even today's standards.[13]

- The Council of Mothers decided critical tribal matters and even nominated the male leaders.
- All real property, both land and dwellings, belonged to the women.
- Compensation for a woman's life required twice the amount of money as that for a male's.
- Women approved punishment for prisoners of war.

Guided purely by arrogance, the Europeans could muster little respect for the Red man. A Dutch clergyman who spent seven years trying to convert the "savages" to the Christian plunder-god describes his prey: "They are very stupid," he wrote in 1644, "I sometimes cannot make them understand what I want." The sanctimonious critic castigated the Indians for their "slovenly dress, failure to bathe, immorality, and cruelty toward their enemies." Another Dutchman felt similarly. They are "as thievish and treacherous as they are tall; and in cruelty they are altogether inhuman, more than barbarous, far exceeding the Africans." Not satisfied, he continued: "I find them entirely savage and wild, strangers to all decency,...uncivil and...proficient in all wickedness and godlessness." Another called them "wild and untamed, reckless, unrestrained, haughty, and more addicted to...cursing and swearing."[14]

These contemptuous words served to excuse the brutal subjection of the "heathens," the commandeering of their trade, and the theft of their land. But it was the introduction of alcohol that sealed the Red man's fate. The Indians had developed an addiction to the drug, and after furs, the traffic in liquor was to them the most important. Prior to the Dutch invasion, the Indians had no experience with intoxicants, preferring to imbibe clear river water. Never missing an opportunity to cheat their Red hosts, some settlers sold watered-down brandy to the Indians, creating additional tensions which often resulted in physical conflict.[15]

The very survival of the newcomers was a result of the superior skills of the New York Indians. The Europeans were quick to assimilate those skills into their own regime before they commenced with the Holocaust in earnest.

Land Theft and New York Barbarism

There was often difficulty in enforcing the order to pay an Indian for the land a settler of the company bought...[16]

Back in Europe, the Dutch investors were encouraging colonization of the new territory, promising to make "masters" of people who would bring fifty settlers to the colony. They would be awarded as much Indian land as they could cultivate and absolute, lordly control over the adults who bound themselves to serve terms ranging from one to six years—the first and mildest form of slavery practiced in New York.[17]

Though the $24 "Manhattan transfer" was the most famous of real estate deals, it paled in comparison to the 1630 "purchase" of more than 700,000 acres, which included the present counties of Albany and Rensselaer, a part of Columbia County, and even a strip in Massachusetts. The Dutchman paid for it with knives, axes, wampum, and cloth, but the new "owner" himself neither lived on nor even visited his estate.[18]

There is no doubt that what the Europeans thought of as "ownership" of land had no place in the Indian belief system. To the Red man, it was the height of arrogance to "own" a creation of the God. To partake of its bounty was a solemn affair. That concept was expressed by the Sauk chief Black Hawk when he wrote long after the crime of exclusive landownership was committed by the European:

My reason teaches me that land *cannot be sold*. The Great Spirit gave it to his children to live upon, and cultivate, as far as is necessary for their subsistence; and so long as they occupy and cultivate it, they have the right to the soil....Nothing can be sold, but such things as can be carried away.[19]

To the Indians, the European was plainly carried away with the plunder demanded by an insatiable foreign power, contorting every supreme law to justify his ungodly ends. By mid-century the Manhattan Island's Native American population had been halved. In 1650, in the midst of the Red Holocaust, Adriaen van der Donck wrote plainly of the onslaught:

We are also in the highest degree beholden to the Indians, who not only have given up to us this good and fruitful country, and for a trifle yielded us the ownership, but also have enriched us with their valuable trade, so that there is no one in New Netherland...without obligation to them. Great is our disgrace now, and happy should we have been, had we acknowledged these benefits as we ought, and had we striven to impart as much as was in our power, to the Indians, the Eternal Good, in return for what they divided with us. It is to be feared that at the Last Day they will stand up against us for this injury. Lord of Rulers! forgive us for not having conducted therein more according to our reason...[20]

It must be kept in mind that the newly conquered territory was governed entirely by the private for-profit Dutch West India Company whose aims, goals and interests did not necessarily coincide with those of the Dutch monarchy. The *Company* settled New York—not the monarchy. It was a corporate venture that did not even answer to the Dutch king. The 19 Company board members back in Holland ran the show in New York and they answered only to the shadowy investors.

William Kieft: The First Nazi?

A succession of debased Dutch rulers lorded over the new settlement on behalf of the Company and the first of this lot was William Kieft. His job was to maintain order and render New Netherland profitable. He failed on both accounts.

Kieft began his dictatorship by imposing a tax on the peaceable Indians. The move immediately angered both Indians and settlers, who depended upon Indian goodwill for the vital fur trade. Kieft arrogantly persisted and proceeded to prosecute a series of wars against the Indians designed to establish one central religious and social doctrine— unchallenged white supremacy.[21]

The Atrocities Begin

Next, we recount a series of atrocities committed under Kieft's reign that have, for the most part, been removed from the history books.

The Dutch Swine Massacre of 1640   The Raritan Indians on Staten Island had reportedly killed some pigs and stolen others from island farmers. In what must be the most noble recorded defense of swine, a hundred soldiers were dispatched to the scene, where they then killed a number of the Indians. The Dutch pork protectorate captured the chief's brother and tortured him "in his private parts with a piece of split wood."

The Raritans retaliated by killing the Staten Island farm workers and claimed, probably justifiably, that it was really white men who had stolen the pigs and charged the deed to the Indians. The practice of blaming the illegal acts of white people on Indians is a known tactic that has no doubt clouded many a history book with inaccurate information. The famous Boston Tea Party, for example, was carried out by Bostonians *dressed as Indians* so that British reprisals for this "revolutionary act" would target innocent local Indians.

But Kieft had no intention to investigate and offered a reward for every Raritan head. Amazingly, not all the neighboring Indians were unfriendly. "One of them walked into Fort Amsterdam two months later carrying a dead man's hand on a stick. It was the hand, he told Kieft, of the chief of the men who killed the farmers on Staten Island. He said he had taken revenge on behalf of the Dutch, 'who were his best friends.'"[22]

1641   In 1641 a Swedish settler was killed by an Indian near what is now Yonkers. Kieft assembled the Dutch West India Company's Black slaves, arming each of them with "a small ax and half pike," and sent them to "harass" their Red brothers.

The Indian warrior, when apprehended, explained that in 1626, as a small boy, he had seen his uncle murdered by Dutchmen on Manhattan and that his act was righteous retaliation. The local chief agreed and refused to turn the brave over to the Dutch, adding that he was "sorry that twenty Christians had not been murdered."

Eighty white men set out from the Dutch fort to burn down the tribe's village and to kill anyone they could get their hands on. They soon got lost and had to return to New Amsterdam. But the expedition was spotted by the Indians, who then chose to negotiate a peace treaty signed in the home of Jonas Bronck, for whom the Bronx is named.[23]

1642-1643   The raids and retaliations multiplied. In 1642 a Dutchman murdered a Hackensack Indian in order to steal his beaver skins. Two Dutchmen were then killed by the Indians in revenge.

In the summer of 1643, a band of English intruders were confronted by the Indians. The freedom fighters came upon the house of Anne Hutchinson (for whom the parkway is named), burned it to the ground, subdued the resistance but spared the youngest daughter, whom they carried off to live with them.

The next stop was the Throckmorton settlement, which the Red fighters destroyed entirely, leaving, to survive, only a remnant of its name in the form of Throggs Neck.[24]

Pavonia Massacre Kieft's Indian policy knew no bounds. By his orders Dutch soldiers slaughtered forty Indians in February of 1643. Another squad proceeded to what is now Jersey City, and murdered 120 Indians in what is known as the Pavonia Massacre.[25]

Dutch soldiers snatched Indian children from their mothers' breasts and hacked the infants to death. Babies were bound to planks, tortured, and then murdered. Still other Indian children had been thrown into the river by the cruel Dutchmen. When those Indians who had escaped the onslaught returned the next morning,

> [they] were murdered in cold blood and tossed into the fire or the water. Some came to our people in the country with their hands, some with the legs cut off, and some holding their entrails in their arms, and others had such horrible cuts and gashes, that worse than they were could never happen.[26]

The soldiers severed the heads of their victims, very likely playing kickball with some of them. A delighted William Kieft decorated the beasts, as eleven outraged Algonquin tribes arose in full-scale war. As one historian has written, "[they] did their ferocious best to wipe the white man off the face of the earth." Before long only three farms on Manhattan and two on Staten Island remained untouched. White men were called in from all over New England, ignoring their differences to eradicate the Red "menace."[27]

In December, Indians near Greenwich "had attacked a party of Christians" (the euphemism for white people), and Kieft felt obliged to send a force of 120 men, who murdered or captured 20 of the Red landowners. Another party of 65 white men killed still more people and burned a good deal of the Indians' winter corn supply.[28]

1 6 4 4   Finally, in the spring of 1644, an expedition led by Captain John Underhill of Massachusetts descended upon a village near today's Greenwich, Connecticut, killing 500 to 700 men, women, and children in the midst of their annual Green Corn Festival. They set fire to the Indian wigwams with men, women and children in them:

> The Indians tried every means to escape, not succeeding in which they returned back to the flames preferring to perish by the fire than to die by our hands.[29]

Only eight Indians escaped the bloody carnage, with the English losing only 15. This brutal attack was the actual reason for the first Thanksgiving. The colonial leaders often proclaimed days of Thanksgiving after successful Indian slaughters, and this one caused great white jubilation. Emboldened Dutch forces invaded Westchester County and killed 500 more Red men, women and children. The various Hudson River tribes then sued for peace, signing a treaty with the Dutch on August 30, 1645.[30]

Kieft's Cowardly Demise   William Kieft's thirst for Indian blood came at too high a price for many of the Dutch settlers. Hundreds of whites, unprotected in the New York frontier, had perished in Kieft's murder-fests, but the dictator himself hardly set foot outside of the safety of the walls of the Dutch fort. His cowardice inspired an assassination attempt, which he barely survived. When confronted, the "chicken-hearted" Kieft calmly passed the blame for the unwarranted attacks on the Indians to others. Kieft was lost at sea as he sailed home in 1647 to defend himself against charges of blundering and cowardice.[31]

New York Red Slavery

In New York, chattel slavery first victimized the Red Man. The white man soon came to believe that the only good Indian was one that he could enslave. Red prisoners of the Dutch West India Company's immoral wars were first given to the soldiers as parting gifts on their return to Holland. A 1663 Dutch law, made to encourage white enlistment in the war against the Esopus Indians, promised whites that "whatever Indians they might take prisoners would be their slaves." [32]

Soon, white Manhattanites and Long Islanders relied mainly on Indians for their domestic labor. The colonists first contracted with the Indians as paid laborers, but, as with the "treaties," the Europeans usually evaded payment altogether. The Indians retaliated by helping themselves to Dutch goods, or by simply setting their former employers' houses on fire. [33] According to one study of Native American slavery, there appear to have been more Indian slaves in New York than in any of the other middle colonies. [34]

Thomas Hawsden of Hempstead sold an Indian boy named Will to the butcher Christifor Dene, who then sold him within a few days to Nathaniel Prime. Jacob Wright of Jamaica, James Loper of Easthampton, John Parker of Southampton, John Wick of Bridgehampton, James Parshall of Southold, William Smith of St. George Manor and Thomas Ford of Flushing all bought Native Americans to be their slaves. [35]

Many Indians were tricked into giving their children to white people for religious instruction to later find that their children were sent to other plantations and sold as slaves. So pervasive was the practice that one historian noted that "indeed a free Indian seems finally to have become an uncommon sight." [36]

The laws of New York declared that "Negro, Indian, Mulatto and other slaves" were to be taxed and controlled like any other piece of property. A 1679 resolution "freeing" Indians in the colony apparently meant nothing to the slave-holding whites. [37] As late as 1797, Indian slavery was acknowledged to be a civic right. The Chief Justice of the State Supreme Court of neighboring New Jersey wrote that Native Americans

> have been so long recognized as slaves in our law...that to free...[those] who challenged their status would violate a long-standing principle which protected property rights in the state. [38]

Ultimately, a 1778 law outlawed Indian slavery.[39]

Red Genocide in New York: 1675-1780

The ancient Covenant Chain of friendship between the Six Nations and the whites had become a fetter to bind the Indian, to reduce him to poverty that the white man might prosper. And the Indian might sometimes wonder, in his humiliation, what had become of that old friendship-a friendship that the white man had assured him would last "as long as the sun shall shine or the waters flow."[40]

When the English gained supremacy in 1664, the Red Holocaust was only accelerated. In the midst of the assault on the New York Indians were the hapless Black slaves of the white settlers. They had been introduced into the region from the start of the settlement and were often caught in the middle of the hostilities. Forced into the position of surrogate warriors for the cowardly European, the Blacks took casualties in the upstate clashes. The 1690 Indian War at Schenectady demonstrates the extent to which whites utilized Black slaves in their unjust wars. Eleven Black slaves were killed in the attack and 5 were captured during the Red man's righteous insurgency.[41]

The British strategy focused on devising a web of deceitful land treaties, which were the epitome of immorality. Fees, fraud, and all forms of chicanery and often brutality attended every acquisition of Indian land. In 1755, after suffering nearly a century of British policies, an Oneida leader pointed to a great white land shark from Albany and said:

> Brother. You promised that you would keep this fire place clean from all filth and that no snake should come into this Council Room. That man sitting there...is a Devil and has stole our Lands, he takes Indians slyly by the Blanket one at a time, and when they are drunk, puts some money in their Bosoms, and persuades them to sign deeds.[42]

And he hadn't yet met Sir Jeffrey Amherst. In 1760, British General Amherst's ten thousand-man army ended French rule in North America. But his hatred for the Red man was boundless. It was he who conceived and implemented the strategy to spread smallpox among them. "Could it not be contrived," he queried a subordinate, "to send the smallpox among these disaffected tribes of Indians? We must on this occasion use every stratagem in our power to reduce them." To Amherst, the Indians were "not as a generous enemy, but as the vilest race of beings that ever infested the earth, and whose riddance from it must be esteemed a meritorious act, for the good of mankind. You will therefore take no prisoners, but put to death all that fall into your hands." New York's Indian policy reflected that belief, with full support of the white population.[43]

After the Red man fought alongside George Washington and the American colonists to end British rule in the Revolutionary War, the white man turned his ravenous eyes upon his former ally. The Six Nations Indians held the territory that today includes most of upstate New York, Pennsylvania, and Ohio. One of the first acts of the new "Americans" was to extinguish the title of the Indians to the soil. Under the guise of making this land *more productive* for Indians, their actual plan was to "buy" it from them and give it to whites. The Indians' "lack of sophistication in real estate matters was nothing short of amazing," wrote historian Barbara Graymont. More amazing was the immorality of the white interlopers. Within a few years the various tribes ceded large tracts to the New York province. Indian names mark hundreds of places, including the names of twenty counties and twelve of the state's sixty-odd cities; the Indians themselves–gone.[44]

On September 12, 1788, the New York officials concluded a treaty with the Onondagas which stated: "First, the Onondagoes do cede and grant all their Lands to the People of the State of New York forever...."[45]

"In less than fifteen years, New York State had reduced this mightiest of all Indian confederacies to a nullity." At this point, the Six Nations entered upon a period wherein they were forced onto reservations, with resultant demoralization and social disruption.[46]

The Senecas, Onondagas, Cayugas, Tuscaroras, Oneidas, St. Regis, Stockbridges, Munsees, and Brothertowns were all driven out of New York by yet another fraudulent treaty—the infamous Treaty of Buffalo Creek of 1838. The wording of the 1838 treaty with the New York Indians is diabolical in its attempt to make the reader believe that the Indians desired their own extermination:

> Whereas, the six nations of New York Indians not long after the close of the war of the Revolution, became convinced from the rapid increase of the white Settlements around, that the time was not far distant when their true interest must lead them to seek a new home among their red brethren in the West....at Green Bay in the Territory of Wisconsin...the United States and the Menomonie Indians, concluded in February, 1831, to which the New York Indians gave their assent on the seventeenth day of October 1832...that they all remove to the same, within three years...many who were in favor of emigration, preferred to remove at once to the Indian territory, which they were fully persuaded was the only permanent and peaceful home for all the Indians....

There's more:

> And whereas, the President being anxious to promote the peace, prosperity and happiness of his red children, and being determined to carry out the humane policy of the Government in removing the Indians from the east to the west of the Mississippi, within the Indian territory, by bringing them to see and feel, by his justice and liberality that it is their true policy and for their interest to do so without delay.

After the wars, diseases, broken treaties, slavery and deportation combined to exterminate the New York Indians, Article 4 of the Treaty of 1838 declares, with the customary hypocrisy unique to the white man, that "[p]erpetual peace and friendship shall exist between the United States and the New York Indians."[47]

Notes

[1]Llewelyn Powys, *Henry Hudson* (New York: Harper, 1928), p. 94; E. M. Ruttenber, *History of the Indian Tribes of Hudson's River* (Port Washington, NY, 1872), p. 7.

[2]See Tingba Apidta, *The Hidden History of Washington, DC: A Guide for Black Folks* (Boston: Reclamation Project, 1996), pp. 5-8; Henry H. Kessler and Eugene Rachlis, *Peter Stuyvesant and His New York* (New York: Random House, 1959), p. 30. Disney saw enough magical drama in the affair to make a children's movie about it in 1995 entitled *Pocahantas*.

[3]Powys, *Henry Hudson*, pp. 96-97; Ellis H. Roberts, *New York: The Planting and the Growth of the Empire State*, vol. 1 (New York: Houghton Mifflin, 1904; reprint, New York: AMS Press, 1973), pp. 3, 5.

[4]Powys, *Henry Hudson*, pp. 106-107; Ruttenber, *History of the Indian Tribes*, pp. 8-10.

[5]Ruttenber, *History of the Indian Tribes*, pp. 9-10; Powys, *Henry Hudson*, pp. 96-97: Verazzano wrote: "We found the country on its banks well peopled, the inhabitants not differing much from the others, being dressed out with the feathers of birds of various colours. They came towards us with evident delight, raising loud shouts of admiration, and showing us where we could most securely land with our boat." Ellis Lawrence Raesly, *Portrait of New Netherland* (Port Washington, NY: Friedman, 1965), p. 174: These women companions produced children by the Dutch visitors. Ruttenber, *History of the Indian Tribes*, p. 20: "In disposition they were generous, 'giving away' whatever they had; of their wives they were careful, always leaving them in their boats when they came on ship-board, and their general deportment was such that with them, [Verazzano] says, 'we formed a great friendship.'"

[6]Powys, *Henry Hudson*, pp. 114-15; Ruttenber, *History of the Indian Tribes*, pp. 11-12.

[7]Powys, *Henry Hudson*, pp. 106-107.

[8]Kessler and Rachlis, *Peter Stuyvesant*, p. 31; Powys, *Henry Hudson*, pp. 91-92, 100-101; Ruttenber, *History of the Indian Tribes*, pp. 8-9; See Apidta, *The Hidden History of Massachusetts: A Guide for Black Folks* (Boston: Reclamation Project, 1995), p. 9; Roberts, *New York*, pp. 3, 5: "Esteban Gomez was a Portuguese, who was a mutineer in the fleet of that discoverer who gave his name to the Straits of Magellan....He carried home with him a cargo which included furs and red men for slaves."

[9]Powys, *Henry Hudson*, pp. 113-14.

[10]William Renwick Riddell, "The Slave in Early New York," *Journal of Negro History*, vol. 13, no. 1 (January 1928), p. 54n; Peter Francis, Jr., "The Beads That Did *Not* Buy Manhattan Island," *New York History*, vol. 67 (January 1986), pp. 8, 20; Edward Robb Ellis, *The Epic of New York City* (New York: Coward-McCann, 1966), p. 18.

[11]Francis, "The Beads That Did *Not* Buy Manhattan Island," pp. 9-10.

[12]Raesly, *Portrait of New Netherland*, pp. 171, 189; Henri Van der Zee, *A Sweet and Alien Land: The Story of Dutch New York* (New York: Viking Press, 1978), p. 102; Ruttenber, *History of the Indian Tribes*, p. 23.

[13]Georgiana C. Nammack, *Fraud, Politics, and the Dispossession of the Indians: The Iroquois*

notes, continued

Land Frontier in the Colonial Period (Norman, OK: Univ. of Oklahoma Press, 1969), p. *xvi*; David M. Ellis et al., *A Short History of New York State* (Ithaca, NY: Cornell Univ. Press in cooperation with the N. Y. State Historical Association, 1957), pp. 11, 12.

[14]Michael Kammen, *Colonial New York–A History* (New York: Charles Scribner's Sons, 1975), p. 61; Thomas E. Burke, Jr., *Mohawk Frontier: The Dutch Community of Schenectady, New York, 1661-1710* (Ithaca, NY: Cornell Univ. Press, 1991), pp. 147, 150. But according to Ruttenber, *History of the Indian Tribes*, p. 23, "foul and impertinent language was despised by them."

[15]Nammack, *Fraud, Politics*, p. 8; Van der Zee, *A Sweet and Alien Land*, p. 101; Trelease, *Indian Affairs in Colonial New York: The Seventeenth Century* (Ithaca, NY: Cornell Univ. Press, 1960), p. 70.

[16]Van der Zee, *A Sweet and Alien Land*, p. 103.

[17]Ellis, *History of New York State*, pp. 18-19; Roi Ottley and William J. Weatherby, eds., *The Negro in New York: An Informal Social History* (Dobbs Ferry, NY: Oceana Publications, 1967), p. 3n.

[18]Ellis, *Epic of New York City*, p. 29.

[19]Nammack, *Fraud, Politics*, p. *xv*; Trelease, *Indian Affairs*, pp. 63-64.

[20]Raesly, *Portrait of New Netherland*, p. 187.

[21]Kessler and Rachlis, *Peter Stuyvesant*, pp. 52-53; Esther Singleton, *Dutch New York* (New York: Dodd, Mead, 1909), p. 329.

[22]Kessler and Rachlis, *Peter Stuyvesant*, pp. 53-54; Netherland Chamber of Commerce in America, *The Dutch in New Netherland and the United States* (1909; reprint, San Francisco: R & E Research Assoc., 1970), p. 34.

[23]Riddell, "The Slave in Early New York," p. 62n; Lloyd Ultan, *The Bronx in the Frontier Era: From the Beginning to 1696* (Dubuque, Iowa: Kendall/Hunt, 1993), pp. 29-30; Kessler and Rachlis, *Peter Stuyvesant*, p. 54; Ellis, *Epic of New York City*, pp. 37, 38; James Riker, *Harlem: Its Origins and Early Annals* (Upper Saddle River, NJ: Literature House/Gregg Press, 1970), pp. 138-39.

[24]Ultan, *The Bronx in the Frontier Era*, pp. 34-35.

[25]Netherland Chamber of Commerce, *The Dutch in New Netherland*, p. 35; Trelease, *Indian Affairs*, p. 73.

[26]Kessler and Rachlis, *Peter Stuyvesant*, pp. 57-58; Trelease, *Indian Affairs*, pp. 72-73.

[27]Ellis, *Epic of New York City*, pp. 38-39; Riker, *Harlem*, pp. 141-42; Kessler and Rachlis, *Peter Stuyvesant*, pp. 57-58.

[28]Trelease, *Indian Affairs*, pp. 78-79.

[29]Trelease, *Indian Affairs*, pp. 79-80.

[30]Ellis, *Epic of New York City*, pp. 39-40; Kessler and Rachlis, *Peter Stuyvesant*, pp. 59-60; Trelease, *Indian Affairs*, p. 83; Raesly, *Portrait of New Netherland*, p. 72; Apidta, *Hidden History of Massachusetts*, pp. 16-19; Ultan, *The Bronx in the Frontier Era*, pp. 37-38.

[31]Riker, *Harlem*, pp. 140, 142; Kessler and Rachlis, *Peter Stuyvesant*, p. 58; Ellis et al., *Short History of New York*, p. 23; Ellis, *Epic of New York City*, p. 40; Raesly, *Portrait of New Netherland*, p. 73.

[32]A. Judd Northrup, "Slavery in New York," *State Library Bulletin*, History No. 4 (May 1900), p. 305; Thomas Joseph Davis, "Slavery in Colonial New York City" (Ph.D. diss., Columbia Univ., 1974), p. 75n; Anne Hartell, "Slavery on Long Island," *Nassau County Historical Journal*, vol. 6, no. 2 (fall 1943), p. 67.

notes, continued

[33]Van der Zee, *A Sweet and Alien Land*, pp. 102-103; Singleton, *Dutch New York*, p. 330.

[34]Richard Shannon Moss, *Slavery on Long Island: A Study in Local Institutional and Early African-American Communal Life* (1993), p. 10.

[35]Moss, *Slavery on Long Island*, pp. 10-11.

[36]Edwin Vernon Morgan, "Slavery in New York, with Special Reference to New York City," *Slavery in the States: Selected Essays* (New York: Negro Universities Press, 1969), pp. 23-25; Bernice Marshall, *Colonial Hempstead: Long Island Life Under the Dutch and English* (Port Washington, Long Island, NY: Friedman, 1962), p. 227.

[37]Hartell, "Slavery on Long Island," p. 66; Northrup, "Slavery in New York," p. 305.

[38]Moss, *Slavery on Long Island*, pp. 10-11.

[39]Hartell, "Slavery on Long Island," p. 67.

[40]Barbara Graymont, "New York State Indian Policy After the Revolution," *New York History*, vol. 57 (October 1976), p. 474.

[41]Burke, *Mohawk Frontier*, pp. 123-24.

[42]Nammack, *Fraud, Politics*, p. 17; Ellis et al., *Short History of New York State*, p. 74.

[43]See Alvin M. Josephy, Jr., *The Patriot Chiefs: A Chronicle of American Indian Resistance* (New York: Viking Press, 1958); Francis Parkman, *The Conspiracy of Pontiac* (New York, 1962); Ellis et al., *Short History of New York State*, pp. 58-59.

[44]Graymont, "New York State Indian Policy," pp. 438, 440, 455, 459, 463; Ellis et al., *Short History of New York State*, pp. 17, 58.

[45]Graymont, "New York State Indian Policy," pp. 459-60.

[46]Graymont, "New York State Indian Policy," p. 472; See Anthony F. C. Wallace, *Death and Rebirth of the Seneca* (New York: Knopf, 1970).

[47]Laurence M. Hauptman, "The State's Men, the Salvation Seekers, and the Seneca: The Supplemental Treaty of Buffalo Creek, 1842," *New York History* (January 1997), pp. 52-53; *Treaty of Buffalo Creek of 1838*. For the Treaty of Buffalo Creek (1838), see Charles J. Kappler, comp., *Indian Affairs: Laws and Treaties*, vol. 2 (Washington, DC: U.S.G.P.O., 1904), pp. 537-42. For an account of this fraudulent document, see Henry S. Manley, "Buying Buffalo from the Indians," *New York History*, vol. 27 (July 1947), 313-29.

Black Slavery in New York

Soon after the attempted enslavement of the Red man, Black Africans became the preferred toiler. The Black African was enslaved in New York in the same manner as had become customary in the plantation South. From the bloody beginning of the white man's assault on Manhattan, Blacks were forced to do a job that the Indian eventually refused to do and that the white man had no history of doing—building a civilization for another race of people.[1]

New York slavery existed in three distinct periods of European dominance of the region:[2]

Slavery under	Term	Length
Dutch	1626 to 1664	38 years
British	1664 to 1776	112 years
Americans	1776 to 1827	51 years

From the very beginning the colony suffered from an acute shortage of laborers. The Dutch West India Company tried every angle to establish a workable slavocracy. They first sent over several boatloads of children from European orphanages, but the colonists complained that such children were more accustomed to begging in the streets than doing a hard day's work. Later, English prisoners proved to be simply too lazy. Given the option of working for the Dutch, or living and trading among the hated Indians, the white laborers often chose buckskin. Indians were seen as unreliable and too likely to run away. It was then determined that "Negroes would accomplish more work for their masters, and at a less expense, than farm servants, who must be bribed to go thither by a great deal of money and promises."[3]

The importation of African slaves into New Netherland began with the forced arrival of 11 Angolan males in 1626, the same year Manhattan was "purchased" from the Indians. Shortly thereafter three Black women were kidnapped and sold to willing European buyers. A Dutch official described the Angolans as "thievish, lazy and useless trash."[4]

In the meantime, the Company was encouraging white settlement in the New Amsterdam wilderness by promising a 10 percent discount on the purchase of Africans and providing free exchange of "unsatisfactory Negroes."[5]

The Dutch West India Company had become a major international slave trader composed of pirates, robbing every vessel it could confront on the high seas.[6] Some of those plundered ships held Africans who would end up in New Amsterdam.

The Slave Trade Begins

The colonists of early New York eagerly dove into the profitable business of trading in African slaves. The first known African-slave ship arriving in New Netherland was the *Tamandere*, which in 1646 brought enslaved Blacks, who were sold for pork and peas.[7]

The now desperate labor-starved whites of the colony demanded an adequate supply of Black Africans.[8] The Dutch West India Company, which had a great interest in Brazil, turned to Jewish merchants for relief, but the colony's leaders complained that these slave speculators forced extortionist terms. The arrangement was described in a remarkable passage in *Harpers New Monthly Magazine*, by Thomas A. Janvier:

> In 1647, the Board of Audit advised that the people of New Netherland should be permitted 'to export their produce even to Brazil in their own vessels....and to trade it off there and to carry back slaves in return'; and at the same time the Board proposed that 'orders should be made in Brazil that Jobbers and Jews who buy up the slaves for cash should not sell them on credit at a higher rate than one per cent. a month, the slaves being hypothecated to them for the full amount'—under which wise

and beneficent arrangements, according to the forecast of the Board, it was hoped that the New Netherland might be adequately supplied with laborers, and that 'the slave trade which hath so long lain dormant, to the great damage of the Company, might by degrees be again revived.' But nothing seems to have come of this good plan—possibly because 'the Jobbers and Jews,' by openly accepting and secretly evading the one-per-cent.-a-month order, succeeded in cornering against the New Netherlanders the slave-market of the Brazils.[9]

According to historian Edwin Olson, "it was not until 1655 that slaves were carried to New Netherland in any great number." This date coincides with the arrival of Jews to America after their evacuation from Brazil in 1654. As the primary group specifically named by Company officials as dealers in the Black slave trade, it is significant that the slave trade accelerated from the date of their arrival. Just prior to this, in 1653, Jewish colonists in Curaçao sought permission from Company officials to purchase African slaves *in New Amsterdam* for exportation to Curaçao. Though their request was denied Jewish inhabitants of Curaçao became major traders in that Caribbean outpost.[10]

FOR SALE,
A Healthy, Strong
Negro Wench,
Of about forty years of age, who under-
stands all kinds of House Work—For
farther particulars inquire of the
subscriber. WILLIAM ROOT.
Water-Vliet, July 23, 1798.

Figure 1--*Albany Centinel*, August 3, 1798

Later, under the British, Jews were active in the New York slave trade. In 1717 and 1721, the *Crown* and the *New York Postillion*, owned by Nathan Simson and his associates, sailed into the harbor with a total of 217 enslaved Africans. According to Dr. Jacob Marcus, the shipments were "two of the largest slave cargoes to be brought into New York in the first half of the eighteenth century."[11]

Private entrepreneurs were now being encouraged to engage in the slave trade. The next ten years saw the forced introduction of hundreds of Black Africans into New

Amsterdam for public auction. More ships arrived at New Amsterdam with slave cargoes of naked Black men and women, many of whom died from exposure to the severe climatic change.[12]

Early New York Slave Ships

The acts of barbarity proved upon the slave captains are so extravagant, that they have been attributed to insanity.[13]

Year	Ship	Description of Shipment
1642	La Garce	Brought in "a few" Africans as slaves.
1646	Tamandere a.k.a. Amandare	The first known slave ship carrying Africans arrived in New Netherland. Africans sold for pork and peas.
1652	St. Anthoni	"A lot of forty-five negroes" came in on a privateer which had been captured from a Spaniard.
1652		A Dutch ship landed and sold Black human beings. "Some of these Negroes are already dead; some have run away; some are still on hand..."
1654	Wittepaert or White Horse	Set sail for Guinea and returned in 1655 with an unknown number of Black victims. Blacks sold at auction for about $125 each—a large sum in those times. "Several of the negroes 'were found to have been infected with some fatal disorder'..."
	New Netherland Indian (two trips)	One slaving voyage yielded a "cargo" of thirty-six Africans that arrived at New Amsterdam in 1661.
1659	Sphera Mundi	Sailed from Curaçao to New Amsterdam.
1660	Eyckenboom	Sailed from Curaçao with "horses and Negroes." Only 27 of the 79 horses survived. Of the 20 Africans, one died; the other 19 were "in fairly good condition."
1661	Arms of Amsterdam	From Curaçao, was captured by the British and rerouted to Virginia. An official resolution offered, "at public sale on public account 40 negroes, young and old, male and female, recently arrived from Curaçao; payment to be made in beavers or in beef, pork, wheat or peas."
1664	Sparrow (Musch)	Most of the Africans were sold at public auction.
1664	Gideon	The last Holocaust ship to arrive under Dutch rule. Described as "a very poor assortment" of 300 "half starved" Africans, 9 of whom died during passage.[14]

The Price of Black New Yorkers

In 1644 the Dutch West India Company, which ruled New York (known then as New Netherland), determined that, "Negroes would accomplish more work for their masters and at a less expense than free servants." From then on, African lives could be bought for pork, peas, tobacco, furs, pelts and almost anything else of value to these early New Yorkers. The leasing of Africans was also widely practiced. In 1641 Company Director General Kieft leased a tract of land (on Manhattan Island) "with two Negroes," for five years at an annual rental of 750 pounds of "well-inspected tobacco." The terms called for a reduction in payment if one or both of the Africans were to die. In 1644 another Dutchman leased a Black woman, with payment made in food and clothing. The Company paid back-wages to its officials in African slaves and sometimes paid merchants for supplies, in Black lives. Stuyvesant followed that same policy in paying off a Company debt to the van Rensselaer family by sending a Company slave to their colony of Rensselaerswyck. And on several occasions, he offered to pay for supplies and provisions for the Company's troop detachment with "parcels of slaves."[15]

Eight Dollars Reward.

RAN AWAY from the Subscriber, living at No. 21, Queen-street, New-York, a MULATTO MAN, named SAM, aged about 20 years, of a middling size, dressed in a new blue-sailor jacket, a new double-breasted brown vest, a pair of half worn brown fustian overalls, and a pair of mixed blue and white stockings. He is a good fiddler and fifer; is forward in his behavior, and very talkative; and has a wife and child, who are supposed to be with him, secreted in this city.

Whoever will bring him to the subscriber, shall have the above reward and all reasonable charges.

Masters of vessels and others, are cautioned not to carry off, or harbor the said Mulatto Man.

JOHN KEESE.

Figure 2 - *New York Packet,* December 5, 1789.

The prices for Black human lives were arbitrarily set depending on demand. The documented transactions show that in

- 1626-1647 the average price was $100 to $150.[16]
- 1654 it was $280
- 1655 a cargo went for $125 "a head"
- 1660 a price listed a range of $90 to $180 depending on age
- 1663 an African woman cost $120
- 1664 the best price of the lot brought $240

The British royalty took its cut of the trade in Black flesh. In 1753 they established a tax on the importation of slaves, the amount based on their ages. If the age was in dispute two Justices of Peace were summoned to assess the age of the Black "item."[17]

The Labor of Early New York Slaves

The Black African captives of the Dutch West India Company engaged in an array of tasks, from agricultural work to military defense, under the whip-wielding "Overseer of Negroes." Whenever "heavy work" was called for it was the Africans who performed it, sometimes with the aid of white criminals. On at least one occasion the Company loaned one of these Africans to a northern settlement to execute a criminal condemned to death by its court. Fort Amsterdam, at the southern-most tip of Manhattan, was built by these captives despite the Company's director Peter Stuyvesant's belief that Blacks were incapable of learning the trades. Stuyvesant himself kept thirty to fifty slaves, "his favorite being Old Mingo, who entertained him by playing the fiddle."[18] The cutting of timber and firewood, clearing land, planting and harvesting crops, the building of roads, collecting garbage, and hauling off dead animals that cluttered the city's streets were all tasks assigned to the Africans. They carried buckets of filth from the backyard outhouses of their oppressors and dumped them into the rivers.[19]

As if the forced labor were not torturous enough, Blacks were required to bear arms against their own Red brothers and sisters to defend the intruder colony. In fact, Manhattan's leaders searched the Caribbean slave centers for Blacks that were fit for "the war against the wild barbarians either to pursue them, when they run away or else to carry the soldiers' baggage."[20]

Dutch Racism and Slavery

The harsh slave system was a matter of course for the white European in early New York. Under the Dutch no protest was ever recorded against the African or Indian slavery.[21] Slave owners and traders enjoyed the honor and respect of their fellow white citizens, with the vast profits easing any potential discord. Their poetry enshrined their evil:

> Glass beads, and brandy, and scissors and knives,
> And other cheap trash for them giving,–
> The profit at least eight hundred per cent,
> If I keep the half of them living.
> For fetch I three hundred blacks alive
> To the port of Rio Janeiro,
> 'T is a hundred ducats apiece for me,
> From the house of Gonzales Perreiro.[22]

Slave labor was indispensable, after all, and whites rallied to its defense religiously, economically and physically. Slave holding became wide spread, even among the clergy, and the citizens of Hempstead, for example, considered the slaves to be "as precious as gold."[23]

But white historians have always tried to downplay the dependence of early New York on Black slavery. The brevity with which they address the subject usually includes some form of exoneration of its New York practitioners, as with this passage by J. H. Innes:

> The negroes settled down into house and farm servants; the relations between them and their masters were usually of a somewhat patriarchal nature, manumissions were frequent, and sincere attachment was often manifested on both sides.[24]

Conveniently ignored is the brutality that always accompanied enslavement of the African. Blacks imported directly from Africa were considered rebellious and difficult to control. The Dutch developed a process called "seasoning," which entailed the "breaking" of Africans on the island of Curaçao before transport to New York. This "breaking" of their will to resist enslavement included unspeakable psychological and physical punishment which, if survived, often made docile the once mighty and proud African.[25]

The Dutch had little compassion for the Blacks they enslaved, earning a reputation as cruel and vicious. The case of Nicolaes

T O   B E   S O L D,
A STOUT NEGRO GIRL, about fix-teen years of age, lately from the coun-ty. Enquire at No. 46, Water-Street.   2 99

TWO GUINEAS REWARD,
RUN AWAY from the fubfcriber on the 23d inftant, a NEGRO MAN named JUBA, about 20 years of age, five feet eight or nine inches high, well built, of a yellowish complexion, fpeaks good Englifh, and is not very talkative:—Had on when he went away, a dark grey broadcloth coat, felt hat and boots. Whoever will apprehend faid Negro, and deli-ver him to me the fubfcriber, or to Mr. Com-fort Saads in New-York, fhall be entitled to the above reward, and all reafonable charges paid.
FRED. J. WHITING.
Danbury, July 2, 1784.
N. B. It is thought the above-mentioned NEGRO is lurking about the city of New-York, in order to procure a paffage to North-Carolina.

Figure 3 - *New York Packet*, July 5, 1784

Boot is illustrative of this character. He appeared in court in New Amsterdam, complaining that the female slave he had bought at a "publick auction" for 230 guilders had died the following day.

> The slave had seemed odd, shouting all the way to her new owner's home. "She could not well hold her feet," a witness told the court, and "her eyes standing fixed in her head," she had

asked for "More, more." A passerby had explained that she was drunk, but the surgeon who was later called had told Boot she was dying, which indeed happened at nine o'clock.[26]

More than a century later under American control, the Dutch reputation still firmly applied. A Frenchman traveling in America in the 1790s, concluded that the Dutch "treat their slaves miserably." When, in 1790, a manumission bill failed to pass the legislature, it was claimed that the abolition measure was opposed by "a great body of Dutch, who hold slaves in this government."[27]

Manumission in Dutch New York

The hogs have eaten all my corn, the slaves have eaten all my hogs, and all I've got left is niggers.[28]

The early manumission of Black slaves is often reported by historians as proof of a kinder, gentler slave system. But what appears to be an act of magnanimity towards loyal Black slaves is, upon closer examination, an act of selfish white opportunism. The first of the Black imports were, indeed, given a measure of independence after 20 years of uncompensated service to the Company, but it was a "freedom" that could be revoked if certain conditions were not met. The first sentence of the 1644 proclamation is the one which white historians remember best:

> Therefore we, the Director and Council do release, for the term of their natural lives, the above named and their wives from Slavery, hereby setting them free and at liberty, on the same footing as other free people here in New Netherland where they shall be able to earn their livelihood by Agriculture, on the land shown and granted to them...

So far, so good. The next part of the order is what they ignore:

> ...on condition that they...shall be bound to pay for the freedom they receive, each man for himself annually, as long as he lives, to the West India Company or its Deputy here, thirty skepels

[barn baskets—22 1/2 bushels] of Maize, or Wheat, Pease or Beans, and one Fat Hog, valued at twenty guilders [$8], which thirty skepels and the hog they, the Negroes, each for himself, promises to pay annually, beginning from the date hereof, on pain, if any one of them shall fail to pay the yearly tribute, he shall forfeit his freedom and return back into the said Company's Slavery....

Followed by an even more profound hypocrisy:

....With express condition, that their children at present born or yet to be born, shall be bound and obligated to serve the Hon'ble West India Company as Slaves. Likewise that the above mentioned men shall be obliged to serve the Hon'ble West India Company here, by water or on land, where their services are required, on receiving fair wages from the Company.[29]

No more deceptive "freedom" has ever been devised, with the possible exception of the Indian treaties and Lincoln's so-called Emancipation Proclamation of a later time.

As plainly deceptive as this document is to Black eyes, here is how Morton Wagman, "a reputable historian," recounts this arrangement. Note how he masks the wretched reality with a term of his own invention—"freedom dues":

In 1644, a group of eleven company slaves...petitioned Director Kieft for their freedom....As part of their freedom dues, they all received plots of farmland on Manhattan...which became the first free black community in New York.[30]

Later in 1662, Stuyvesant "freed" three women slaves *on condition that one of them do housework for him each week.* A few months later, he "freed" an "old and sickly Negress" who had been in the Company's service for over thirty-five years. The manumission of elderly slaves is actually evidence of the cruelty of a heartless master who would turn a senior citizen out on her own (without recompense) after decades of service and in her waning years. Shortly afterward, in December 1663, about eight or nine slaves, possibly the last Blacks remaining in the Company's service, were granted this so-called "half liberty."[31]

The granting of this new oxymoronic status, called *manumitted slavery*, had still another level of selfish motivation. By 1644, it had become too expensive to maintain a large supply of slaves for intermittent use. Unlike the plantation South, the northern planting season was abbreviated by weather conditions, leaving an extended idle time for the agricultural laborers. They, nonetheless, had to be fed, housed, clothed and guarded throughout this "unproductive" period. The Company devised this "half-freedom" purely for purposes of economic efficiency. Such status forced the Black slaves to fend for themselves until they were needed again on a full-time basis. But that is not all. Unrepentant Indian warriors were burning houses, cattle, barns and crops, and killing and capturing farmers and their families, so the Dutch began granting farmland to freed Blacks, positioning them as a buffer zone between the hostile Red neighbors and the white settlements, in what is today Harlem.[32]

Slavery and Religion in Early New York

No one can seriously argue that the religious community of New York ever crusaded to ameliorate the conditions of their Black brethren. Instead, devout whites collectively searched the gospel for, and often found, vindication of slavery, of genocide and of Jim Crow. As far as Blacks

☞ For Sale, a NEGRO MAN 19 years old—it being his wish to be sold. He may be exchanged for a negro woman. Apply as above.
15th March.

To be SOLD for the term of 12 years,
A MULATTO BOY about 15 years of age; is strongly and healthy, and accustomed to all kinds of house work. Inquire of the Printers.

FOR SALE.
A Smart, active NEGRO MAN, bred to farming—for some time followed the water, and is a trusty hand on board of a vessel. Inquire of AARON BURKE, no. 123, Broad-street dock.

Figure 4 - *New York Diary*, March 26, 1794

and Indians were concerned, the many cathedrals, churches and synagogues that furnish variety to the New York skyline were monuments to architecture and little more. In fact, Black slavery never even became a "moral issue" until the institution had existed in New York for 200 years.[33]

Despite Peter Stuyvesant's belief in his own divine command ("We derive our authority from God and the West India Company..."), the idea that religion guided the behavior of the settlers is simply myth. The term "Christian" meant "white" to the Europeans and bestowed upon them a natural eminence and excused their every racist policy and act.[34]

Early on, the Dutch Reformed Church busied itself bestowing its blessing on the Dutch West India Company's genocidal policy toward the Indians. What the Europeans thought of as religion was, most assuredly, as foreign to Jesus as it was to the Indians and Blacks who suffered under its devotees. In any case, this was the white man's religion and only halfhearted attempts were made to bring the Company-owned "heathen" into the light—even though, according to an early Dutch minister, "they have no faculty of comprehension." This, in no way, meant to suggest any form of physical, spiritual or legal equality, but it did mean that Blacks were asked to submit to yet another layer of authority for no good purpose.[35]

New York's religious leadership took seriously the job of sanctifying race hatred. An Anglican leader preached "that a Negro hath no soul [nor does he] possess potentially the same intellectual powers as the whites." Even when Africans succumbed to efforts at conversion, others in the clergy balked: "As to baptisms," one minister wrote in 1664,

> the negroes occasionally request that we should baptize their children, but we have refused to do so, partly on account of their lack of knowledge and of faith, and partly because of the worldly and perverse aims on the part of said negroes. They wanted nothing else than to deliver their children from bodily slavery, without striving for piety and Christian virtues.[36]

Certainly, the wary slavemasters resisted these conversion efforts mightily, believing that *any* form of education for Blacks was bad for white authority. The government sought to allay this concern by passing an act in 1706 which declared, "That the baptizing of any Negro, Indian or Mulatto Slave shall not be any cause or reason for setting them or any of them at liberty."[37]

Their missionaries to the Indians were equally pessimistic: "We have had one Indian here with us full two years," wrote the Rev. Samuel Drisius in 1659,

> We likewise presented him with a Bible in order to work through him some good among the Indians. But it all resulted in nothing. He has taken to drinking of Brandy; he pawned the Bible and became a real beast who is doing more harm than good among the Indians.[38]

But these conversion efforts were cynical from the start. Rev. Jonas Michaëlius, after only four months among the Red "heathen," thought that

Ten Dollars Reward.

RUN AWAY from the Subscriber, on the 24th inst. a NEGRO MAN named PETER, about 22 years or age, 5 feet 7 inches high, of a yellow complexion: Had on when he went away, a brown coloured coat, a blue and grey mixed coloured weltcoat, a brown linen trowsers, and an English castor hat: He likewise took with him, a grey coat, leather breeches, and striped linen trowsers---it is supposed he will change his habit: --He talks English and Dutch, and if particular notice is taken of him in his walking his knees stand back more than common. Whoever takes up and secures said negro, so that his master may get him again, shall receive the above reward, and all reasonable charges, paid by   EVERT W. SWART.
Fish Kill, Sept. 26.   24   3

TAKEN UP, by the Subscribers, a bout a fortnight since, a NEGRO MAN, of a dark yellow complexion, who calls himself JIM, about 5 feet 6 or 7 inches high, supposed to be about 29 years of age: He has a remarkable scar of a burn on his buttock, and also several others on the lower part of his leg, and a ridge on his great toe. It is supposed that he belongs to some part of Virginia, and appears to answer a description given of a runaway, in a late advertisement, signed William Fitzhugh, of Boyo's Hole, King George county, Virginia. The owner of said Negro, can have him again, by applying at the New Gaol, of the city of New York, paying the offered reward and charges, to
JAMES CAMPBELL,
Mayor's Marshall.
NICH. COONRAD, Constable,
West Ward.

Wanted immediately to Hire,

A white Woman (or Negro Wench) who are single, and have no children, and who understand cooking, washing, and house-work, for a small family. They must be well recommended. Enquire of the Printer.   24

A NEGRO BOY,

Is wanted to be purchased,
Of about 17 or 19 years of age,
Who has been brought up to Family or House-Work.
Enquire of the Printer.   24 3

Figure 5 - *New York Packet*, September 30, 1784.

"[e]veryone conversant with the Indians in and around New Netherland will be able to say that it is morally impossible to convert the adults to the Christian faith." He was hardly likely to bring any of his Algonquin subjects to Jesus, especially since he thought them to be

> entirely savage and wild, strangers to all decency, yea, uncivil and stupid as garden stakes, proficient in all wickedness and ungodliness, devilish men, who serve nobody but the Devil....I have as yet been able to discover hardly a single good point...[39]

The good reverend's Hitlerian solution was to kidnap the Indian children, erasing from their minds any memory of their culture and beliefs. After all, these were firm believers in the Hamitic Myth, an invention of Medieval Jewish rabbis that advanced the notions that the Africans were black because they were cursed by God and that they were destined to be servants of white people. Such a belief system justified the most horridly racist behavior and motivated the Red and Black Holocausts.[40] In 1708 the Rev. Muirson, an English missionary, failed to convince his Red subjects of their Hamitic duties:

To be SOLD, or exchanged for a handy BOY, from 15 to 17 years old,

A STOUT YOUNG NEGRO MAN, ufed to farming. The proprietor having no ufe for faid Negro, is the reafon he is to be parted with. Inquire of the Printer.

Figure 6 - *New York Journal*, March 25, 1784.

> I have taken some pains to teach some of them, but to no purpose, for they seem regardless of instruction. And when I have told them of the evil consequences of their hard drinking, etc., they replied that Englishmen do the same; and that it is not so great a sin in an Indian as in an Englishman, because the Englishman's religion forbids it, but an Indian's does not. They further say they will not be Christians, nor do they see the necessity for so being, because we do not live according to the precepts of our religion....I am heartily sorry that we should give them such a bad example, and fill their mouths with such objections against our blessed religion.[41]

Mockery of Native religion and culture extended also to the African slave, who struggled to get a spiritual bearing amid his New York hell. From the earliest times, the Church refused to perform marriages, burial rites or sick visits for Blacks in New York. In fact, although slave labor built the great Trinity Church in 1679, a law was soon passed "that no Negro shall be buried" there. One observer commented on the funerals of Black people:

Ten Dollars Reward,

RUN away from the Subscriber, living at Seacaucus, State of New-Jerſey, a NEGRO MAN, named TOM, twenty-one yeaɩs of age, about five feet eight inches high, very Black, and has no partïcular Mark. Had on when he went away Tow Trowſers about half worn, a new Tow Shirt, and without Stockings or Shoes. He took with him two Jackets, a ſmall reamed black Hat.—Whoever takes up ſaid Negro, and delivers him to JOSEPH SMITH, in New-York, near Dean's Diſtillery, ſhall receive the above Reward, and all reaſonable Charges paid.   DANIEL SMITH. *July* 11, 1786.

Figure 7 - *Independence Journal*, July 19, 1786.

[P]erhaps some ridiculous heathen rites were performed at the grave by some of their own people...[F]requent discourses were made in conversation [amongst whites] that [Blacks] had no souls and perished as beasts. [42]

By 1800, the Church had "warmed up" to the Black population, and the highly esteemed pastor Dominie Lansing offered them advice, opening with: "Now niggers and nigger wenches I have a word for you." Then he reminded them of their duty "faithfully to serve and obey their masters."[43]

Black and Red: Natural Allies

The relationship between the two darker peoples of the region was complicated by the role the European demanded that each one play in the growth of his white settlement. Whites made it a crime for Indians to harbor runaway slaves or to even associate with them—which circumvented any mass unity. The Minisinks on eastern Long Island nevertheless helped "fugitive" Africans during the early eighteenth century and provided the runaways with weapons to return and fight for the freedom of their brethren still in captivity. One such band of freedom fighters became so menacing by 1702 that Governor Edward Cornbury ordered local authorities to "fire on them [and] kill or destroy them if they cannot otherwise be taken." Treaties were established with extradition clauses to thwart this apparently common practice.[44]

Violent confrontations sometimes were reported between the Black man and the Red man, but always in the context of the European's oppressive racial environment. The ongoing war of genocide against the Indians brought retaliation from the Indian, who sometimes killed the white man and his Black captives. Generally, Blacks fleeing from European oppression could count on their Red brothers for assistance. In defiance of diplomatic pressures, the Iroquois "almost never returned fugitive slaves who had come to them for help."[45]

By the time of the British military invasion of 1664, which unseated the Dutch and renamed the colony "New York," the business of Black slavery was booming, with the Black population reaching nearly 700—7% of the total. Remarkably, the defeated Dutch leader Peter Stuyvesant blamed the colony's newly arrived Black victims for the Dutch loss of Manhattan. The *Gideon* had in its hold what Stuyvesant described as "a very poor assortment" of 300 Africans. He blamed his hasty surrender of the colony on the diminished food supply because of the untimely arrival of so many sick and "half starved" slaves.[46]

Slave Merchants & Slave Ships: The British

> *"I could tell you," said a merchant to us the other day, "of at least twenty firms who are more than suspected of a connection with the Cuban importation of Africans."*[47]

New York's robust slave trade reached its peak in the early 1760s. White New Yorkers traded directly to Africa and continued to be active in the traffic down to the eve of the American Revolution. The British monarchy instructed

Governor Hunter to provide a steady supply of Africans for the colony. The population of enslaved Africans thus increased from around 2,100 in 1698 to almost 20,000 by 1771, making it the largest slave population north of Maryland. As James Lydon stated, "the large number of vessels returning direct from Africa indicates a strong local demand for slaves."[48]

The following is an abbreviated list of slave ships that docked at New York Harbor between 1715 and 1765: [49]

Abigail	Cornelia	George	Jolly	Pelican	Society
Abraham	Crown	Georgia	Judith & Rebecca	Penellopy	Speedwell
Africa	Crown Gally	Georgia Pacquet	June & Hester	Peter	Squirrel
Albany	Dart	Glassco	Katherina	Peter & John	St. &rew
Allida	Delight	Good Intent	Katherine	Phillipsburg	St. Andrews
Ancram	Diamond	Grayhound	King George	Phoebe	St. Michael
Ann	Dighton	Greenwich	Lady Anne	Pinetree	St. Peter
Anna	Dolphin	Griffin	Lamb	Polly	Stanhope
Anne	Don Carlos	Hamilton	Lancashire	Portsmouth	Stephen
Anne & Cathrine	Dove	Hampstead	Lark	Prince Frederick	Success
Anne & Elisa	Dragon	Happy	Legunea	Prince George	Susanah
Anne & Eliza	Duke of Port'd	Happy Return	Little Marys	Prince William	Swallow
Anne & Elizabeth	Duke of Portl&	Hawk	Loyallty	Princes	Temperance
Anne & Judith	Eagle	Henry	Lyon	Princess Ann	Hester
Anne & Mary	Ebenezer	Heron & Dolphin	Marg't & Mary	Prospect	Thomas
Antigoa	Elisabeth	Hester	Margaret	Providence	Thos. & Mary
Antigua	Eliz. & Anne	Hope	Mary	Prudence	Three Bros.
Arent	Eliza	Hopewell	Mary & Anne	Prudent Betty	Three Friends
Benja'n	Eliza & Martha	Hum bird	Mary & Ellinor	Rachel & Anne	Torbay
Bettsey	Eliza & Mary	Hunter	Mary & Hannah	Ranger	Trial
Bird	Elizabeth	Huntington	Mary & Marg't	Rebecca	True Blue
Black Eyd Susan	Elizabeth & Mary	Illustrious	Mary Anne	Retrieve	Tryall
Black Joke	Endeavour	Industry	Midnight	Revenge	Turtle Dove
Blessing	Enterprize	Jacob	Morning Star	Richmond	Two Brothers
Blk Ey'd Susan	Essex	Jamaica	Nassau	Riddle	Two Friends
Bruce Hope	Esther	James	Neptune	Rope	Two friends
Brunswick	Exchange	James & David	Nevis	Rose	Two Sisters
Burnett	Expedition	James & Henry	New Brunswick	Royal Ranger	Union
Byam	Fairfield	Jane	NY Postillion	Royall Anne	Unity
Caracoa	Fancy	Jean	Newbery	Ruby	Virgin
Cath'n & Mary	Fanny	Jenny	Nightingale	Sally	Wall
Catherine	four Sisters	Jno. & Cathrine	Nights Ramble	Samuel	Walter
Catherine & Mary	Fran. & Cathrine	Jno. & Eliza	Nonsuch	Sarah	Warwick
Charity	Frances	Jno. & Mary	Norris	Sarah & Elizabeth	Westmorl&
Charlotta	Francis	Jo'n & Eliz.	Oglethorpe	Sea Flower	Weymouth
Charlotte	Francis & Cathrine	Joanna	Old Soldier	Sea Horse	Wheel of Fortune
Charm'g Betty	Free Mason	Johanna	Olive Branch	Sea Nymph	William
Charm'g Philas	Friends Adventure	John	Oswego	Seaflower	William & Thomas
Charm'g Sally	Friendship	John & Anne	Overplus	Seahorse	York
Charming Joanna	Garret	John & Catherin	Patience	Sincerity	Younger Brother
Content	Gen'l Monckton	John & Mary	Pearl	Small Gains	

RUN away on the fourth of February *laſt, from* Robert James Livingſton, *a tall likely Negro Wench, named* Nell, *al⁴ₐt 36 Years of Age : Had on when ſhe went away, a blue Pennſlon Petticoat, a ſhort blue and white homeſpun Gown, with a ſhort blue Duffils Cloak and Straw Bonnet ; ſhe is mark'd with nine Spots on each Temple, and nine on her Forehead. Whoever takes up ſaid Wench, ſo that her Maſter may have her again, ſhall have* Twenty Shillings *Reward, and all reaſonable Charges, paid by*

ROBERT JA. LIVINGSTON.

Figure 8 - *New York Gazette*, March 5, 1749.

To be Sold by OBADIAH WELLS, in *Prince's-Street*, *A Likely Negro Boy, about* 20 *Years of Age,* is well recommended, and ſuitable for either Town or Country ; alſo a parcel of Cordage. Spunyarn, Iron Pots, and ſundry ſorts of European Goods : Likewiſe a quantity of ſquare Timber, ſhort Cedar Shingles for ſtripping off, and ſix Foot Cedar Claphoards; Glaziers Lead, Bar, Sheet, White and Red ditto, Spaniſh Brown, Verdegreaſe, Indian Red, Spruce Yellow ; and divers ſorts of other Colour's ; Glaſs by wholeſale or retail ; where all ſorts of glazier's Work and Painting, is done : He likewiſe gives ready Money for Hogs Briſtles.

TO BE SOLD, A Young Wench about 29 Years old, that drinks no Strong Drink, and gets no Children ; a very good Drudge : Enquire of the Printer hereof.

Figure 9 - *New York Gazette*, January 30, 1748.

Piracy & Smuggling

It would surprise most New Yorkers to know that piracy was a major industry in the city. The notorious William Kidd, a New York City privateer, operated with impunity in New England waters and most likely buried treasure on the Long Island shore. Piracy and the smuggling of kidnapped Black Africans into New York were popular and profitable ventures of the most prominent New York merchants.[50] It became so pervasive that the government was forced to action:

> It has been credibly represented that a great number of Slaves have clandestinely been imported into this colony both by Land and Water, to the great impairing of the Duty laid on them, and to the great Discouragement of fair Traders.[51]

The De Lancey and Philipse dynasties accumulated much of their wealth by piracy. Pirates operating on the African coast were supplied by New York merchants, who were there to trade for African citizens. It was Frederick Philipse, the merchant, slave-trader and politician, who admitted, "It is by negroes that I find my chiefest profit."[52] According to one historian of piracy,

> New York provided the headquarters for the pirate trade....as early as the year 1692 piracy and illegal trade were adopted as "the beloved twins of the merchants of New York." The new governor, Benjamin Fletcher, was most guilty.

The good governor openly welcomed notorious pirates, "accepting from them presents of gold and even of ships in return for immunity from arrest."[53]

The Americans: Slave Ships From New York

Slave ships sailed in and out of New York harbor unabated under the British and then the Americans long after the trade had been "outlawed." The enormous profits attracted merchants of every description and the city became "a major center for illegal slavers." Slave smugglers, called "blackbirders," were so commonplace that they often met at Sweet's Restaurant on Fulton Street to trade tales of their wicked schemes. Even the New York Yacht Club sailed a slave ship.[54]

The *Anti-Slavery Standard* newspaper of July 7, 1860, succinctly stated the following:

> [T]here is no question but that New York city is the great slave-ship mart of this continent. It is here that slavers are bought, owned and fitted out, and the threads to all the ramifications of this nefarious traffic are held by New York merchants...It is well known that over sixty vessels of different rigs leave this port every year....It can hardly be conceived that the officers whose duty it is to prevent the departure of these vessels can be doing their duty.

Even though such commerce carried the death penalty it was known that no one had ever been executed for what amounted to a minor offense. United States District Attorney James I. Roosevelt publicly proclaimed that President James Buchanan would "probably pardon" anyone convicted of illegal slave trading.[55]

A hearty ſtrong Negro WENCH, Sober and honeſt, with two female children, the one four years, the other ſeven ; She was brought up in the country, but has lived ſome time in this city. She will be ſold either with one or both her children, or without, as the purchaſer ſhall chuſe. Enquire of the Printer.

Figure 10 - *New York Packet*, January 29, 1784.

Additionally, many New York merchants claiming to be engaged in legitimate business "are really engaged in furnishing supplies for slavers— men, books, charts, and all the articles needed in the trade."[56]

The *Anti-Slavery Standard* took account of this wicked merchandising of Black Africans and published the names of slaveships that departed from New York and landed their cargoes on the island of Cuba in 1859 and 1860:

Ship	Captain & Cargo
Orion*	Capt. Morgan (800 Africans)
J. Harris	Capt. Steele (550 Africans)
Pamphylion	unknown (700 Africans)
Wildfire	Capt. Stanhope (507 Africans)
Wm. G. Lewis	Capt. Faulkner (411 Africans)
Panchita	Capt. Stanhope
Ysla de Cuba	Capt. Larkin
Star of the East	Capt. Hinckley
Laurens	Capt. Curtis
C. H. Sampson	Capt. Davis
Belle	Capt. Stewarts
Charlotte	Capt. Lockhart
Ellen	unknown
Asa Fish	Capt. Dickie
Hungarian	Capt. Dickie
Sultana	Capt. Bowen
Tyrant	Capt. Lind

*The *Orion* was sent to New York but the United States Commissioners found "no proof" against her. Soon thereafter she sailed for the Congo, and again was captured with 800 Black Africans on board.[57]

> It is not to be wondered, that when slaves can be bought for $25 and sold for $1,200, men will engage in this brutalizing trade; and knowing that for an outlay of $15,000 the sum of $720,000 can be realised...[58]

The profits were so great that the vessels could be burned or scuttled, with only a loss of from three to four thousand dollars. A number of vessels sailed from New York during 1855-57. Many others were known to have left during that period, but the following met a cruel end.[59]

Name	Fate
Millanden	Destroyed at sea
Glanmorgan	Captured—condemned at Boston
Silenus	Captured—destroyed on the coast
Gen. Pierce	Captured and condemned
Mary Jane Peck	Captured by the British
Mary E. Smith	Captured by the Brazilians
Advance	Captured—condemned at Norfolk
Julia Moulton	Destroyed at sea
Julia Mystle	Destroyed at sea
Jespar	Captured—acquitted
Chancellor	Captured—not yet decided
Martha	Captured—condemned in New York
Falmouth	Captured—condemned in New York
Horatio	Destroyed at sea
Lady Suffolk	Captured—and since in the Mexican service
Republic	Destroyed at sea
Altivie	Destroyed at sea
N. H. Gambrell	Captured—condemned in New York
Braman	Captured and condemned

Notes

[1] Thomas A. Janvier, "New York Slave-Traders," *Harper's New Monthly Magazine*, January, 1895, p. 293; William Renwick Riddell, "The Slave in Early New York," *Journal of Negro History*, vol. 13, no. 1 (January 1928), pp. 54-55; Darold D. Wax, "Preferences For Slaves In Colonial America," *Journal of Negro History*, vol. 58, no. 4 (October 1973), p. 386.

[2] A. Judd Northrup, "Slavery in New York," *State Library Bulletin*, History No. 4 (May 1900), p. 246.

[3] Anne Hartell, "Slavery on Long Island," *Nassau County Historical Journal*, vol. 6, no. 2 (fall 1943), p. 67; Northrup, "Slavery in New York," pp. 248-49; Edith Evans Asbury, "Freed Black Farmers Tilled Manhattan's Soil in the 1600's," *The New York Times*, 7 December 1977, sec. B; Michael Kammen, *Colonial New York–A History* (New York: Charles Scribner's Sons, 1975), p. 58; Joyce D. Goodfriend, "Burghers and Blacks: The Evolution of a Slave Society at New Amsterdam," *New York History*, vol. 59 (April 1978), p. 127; Edwin Olson, "Negro Slavery in New York, 1626-1827" (Ph.D. thesis,

notes, continued

New York Univ., 1938), pp. 6, 11; Riddell, "The Slave in Early New York," p. 55.

[4]Federal Writers' Project, *New York Panorama* (New York: Random House, 1938; reprint, 1984), p. 132; Richard Shannon Moss, *Slavery on Long Island: A Study in Local Institutional and Early African-American Communal Life* (1993), p. 3; Charles E. Corwin, "Efforts of the Dutch Colonial Pastors for the Conversion of the Negroes," *Journal of the Presbyterian Historical Society*, vol. 12, no. 7 (April 1927), p. 425; Roi Ottley and William J. Weatherby, eds., *The Negro in New York: An Informal Social History* (Dobbs Ferry, NY: Oceana Publications, 1967), pp. 2, 3. Thomas Joseph Davis, "Slavery in Colonial New York City" (Ph.D. diss., Columbia Univ., 1974), p. 22; Edwin Vernon Morgan, "Slavery in New York, with Special Reference to New York City," *Slavery in the States: Selected Essays* (New York: Negro Universities Press, 1969), pp. 3-4.

[5]Davis, "Slavery in Colonial New York City," p. 32.

[6]Janvier, "New York Slave-Traders," p. 293; Moss, *Slavery on Long Island*, p. 12; Olson, "Negro Slavery in New York," p. 3; Ottley and Weatherby, *The Negro in New York*, p. 3; Northrup, "Slavery in New York," p. 248; Henri Van der Zee, *A Sweet and Alien Land: The Story of Dutch New York* (New York: Viking Press, 1978), p. 254; Goodfriend, "Burghers and Blacks," pp. 134-35; Harold C. Syrett, "Private Enterprise in New Amsterdam," *William and Mary Quarterly*, vol. 11, no. 4 (October 1954), p. 537.

[7]Northrup, "Slavery in New York," p. 250; Goodfriend, "Burghers and Blacks," p. 128.

[8]Riddell, "The Slave in Early New York," pp. 58-59.

[9]Riddell, "The Slave in Early New York," p. 56; Janvier, "New York Slave-Traders," p. 294; E. B. O'Callaghan, ed., *Documents Relative to the Colonial History of the State of New York*, vol. 1 (Albany, 1856), pp. 242-48.

[10]Olson, "Negro Slavery in New York," pp. 18-19.

[11]Jacob Rader Marcus, *Early American Jewry*, vol. 1 (Philadelphia: Jewish Publication Society of America, 1951), pp. 64-65. See also *The Colonial Laws of New York*, vol. 1 (Albany, 1894), p. 918.

[12]Goodfriend, "Burghers and Blacks," p. 126; Seth Scheiner, *Negro Mecca* (New York: New York Univ. Press, 1965), p. 1; Davis, "Slavery in Colonial New York City," p. 40; Olson, "Negro Slavery in New York," p. 64.

[13]Charles W. Elliott, *The New England History*, vol. 2 (New York, 1857), p. 174.

[14]Morgan, "Slavery in New York," pp. 6-7; Northrup, "Slavery in New York," pp. 250, 252-53; Goodfriend, "Burghers and Blacks," pp. 128-29, 134, 138, 139, 141; Riddell, "The Slave in Early New York," pp. 59-61; Van der Zee, *A Sweet and Alien Land*, p. 253; Janvier, "New York Slave-Traders," pp. 295, 300-301; Olson, "Negro Slavery in New York," pp. 20n, 23-24; Ottley and Weatherby, *The Negro in New York*, p. 5; Davis, "Slavery in Colonial New York City," p. 42.

[15]Riddell, "The Slave in Early New York," p. 55; Goodfriend, "Burghers and Blacks," p. 133; Van der Zee, *A Sweet and Alien Land*, p. 252; Olson, "Negro Slavery in New York," p. 23; Morton Wagman, "Corporate Slavery in New Netherland," *Journal of Negro History*, vol. 65, no. 1 (winter 1980), p. 37.

[16]Northrup, "Slavery in New York," p. 249.

[17]Hartell, "Slavery on Long Island," p. 56.

[18]Edward Robb Ellis, *The Epic of New York City* (New York: Coward-McCann, 1966), p. 50.

[19]Wagman, "Corporate Slavery in New Netherland," pp. 34-37; Riddell, "The Slave in Early New York," p. 60; Olson, "Negro Slavery in New York," pp. 21-22; Goodfriend,

notes, continued

"Burghers and Blacks," pp. 129-31; Ellis, *Epic of New York City*, p. 48.

[20]Wagman, "Corporate Slavery in New Netherland," p. 35; Northrup, "Slavery in New York," p. 251; Ottley and Weatherby, *The Negro in New York*, p. 12.

[21]Olson, "Negro Slavery in New York," p. 16.

[22]J. H. Innes, *New Amsterdam and Its People: Studies, Social and Topographical, of the Town under Dutch and Early English Rule*, vol. 1 (New York: Friedman, 1969), pp. 43-44.

[23]Goodfriend, "Burghers and Blacks," p. 144; Bernice Marshall, *Colonial Hempstead: Long Island Life Under the Dutch and English* (Port Washington, Long Island, NY: Friedman, 1962), pp. 223-24.

[24]Innes, *New Amsterdam and Its People*, p. 44.

[25]Kammen, *Colonial New York*, pp. 58-59.

[26]Van der Zee, *A Sweet and Alien Land*, p. 253.

[27]Shane White, *Somewhat More Independent: The End of Slavery in New York City, 1770-1810* (Athens, Georgia: Univ. of Georgia Press, 1991), p. 20.

[28]Hartell, "Slavery on Long Island," p. 69.

[29]Northrup, "Slavery in New York," p. 247; Olson, "Negro Slavery in New York," pp. 25-26; Riddell, "The Slave in Early New York," p. 56.

[30]Wagman, "Corporate Slavery in New Netherland," p. 38.

[31]Wagman, "Corporate Slavery in New Netherland," pp. 39-40.

[32]Asbury, "Freed Black Farmers"; Olson, "Negro Slavery in New York," p. 25n; James Riker, *Harlem: Its Origins and Early Annals* (Upper Saddle River, NJ: Literature House/Gregg Press, 1970), p. 202.

[33]David M. Ellis et al., *A Short History of New York State* (Ithaca, NY: Cornell Univ. Press in cooperation with the N. Y. State Historical Association, 1957), p. 67; Northrup, "Slavery in New York," p. 244.

[34]Ellis et al., *Short History of New York State*, p. 18; Winthrop D. Jordan, *White Over Black: American Attitudes Toward the Negro, 1550-1812* (New York: W. W. Norton, 1968), p. 94.

[35]Riddell, "The Slave in Early New York," pp. 57, 65; Morgan, "Slavery in New York," pp. 18-20; Olson, "Negro Slavery in New York," pp. 28-29, 171.

[36]Northrup, "Slavery in New York," p. 245; Moss, *Slavery on Long Island*, p. 21; Sheldon S. Cohen, "Elias Neau, Instructor to New York's Slaves," *New-York Historical Society Quarterly*, vol. 55, no. 1 (January 1971), p. 15; Kammen, *Colonial New York*, p. 22; Corwin, "Efforts of the Dutch Colonial Pastors," p. 429; Thomas E. Burke, Jr., *Mohawk Frontier: The Dutch Community of Schenectady, New York, 1661-1710* (Ithaca, NY: Cornell Univ. Press, 1991), p. 129.

[37]Moss, *Slavery on Long Island*, p. 23; Janvier, "New York Slave-Traders," pp. 303-304; Northrup, "Slavery in New York," p. 257; Olson, "Negro Slavery in New York," pp. 111, 112; Charles W. Baird, *Chronicle of a Border Town: History of Rye, Westchester County, New York, 1660-1870* (New York, 1871; reprint, Harrison, NY: Harbor Hill Books, 1974), pp. 185-86; Riddell, "The Slave in Early New York," pp. 65-66; Cohen, "Elias Neau," p. 17; See also Northrup, "Slavery in New York," p. 258: "...(prevailing also in the Roman law), that one Christian could not, under the law of his religion, hold another Christian in slavery."

[38]Esther Singleton, *Dutch New York* (New York: Dodd, Mead, 1909), p. 187.

[39]Riddell, "The Slave in Early New York," p. 57; Moss, *Slavery on Long Island*, p. 22; Cohen, "Elias Neau," p. 26; Corwin, "Efforts of the Dutch Colonial Pastors," p. 427;

notes, continued

Ellis Lawrence Raesly, *Portrait of New Netherland* (Port Washington, NY: Friedman, 1965), p. 173.

[40]Raesly, *Portrait of New Netherland*, p. 173; Jordan, *White Over Black*, p. 18.

[41]Baird, *Chronicle of a Border Town*, p. 191.

[42]Olson, "Negro Slavery in New York," pp. 77-78, 170; Burke, *Mohawk Frontier*, p. 129; Kammen, *Colonial New York*, p. 60; Carl Nordstrom, "The New York Slave Code," *Afro-Americans in New York Life and History*, vol. 4, no. 1 (January 1980), p. 8; Ottley and Weatherby, *The Negro in New York:*, p. xvii; *Ecclesiastical Records of the State of New York*, vol. 3 (Albany, 1902), p. 1609.

[43]Carl Nordstrom, "Slavery in a New York County," *Afro-Americans in New York Life and History*, vol. 1, no. 2 (July 1977), p. 148; Goodfriend, "Burghers and Blacks," pp. 131-32.

[44]Davis, "Slavery in Colonial New York City," p. 90; Riddell, "The Slave in Early New York," pp. 82-84.

[45]Kenneth W. Porter, "Relations Between Negroes and Indians Within the Present Limits of the United States," *Journal of Negro History*, vol. 17, no. 1 (January 1932), p. 303; Kammen, *Colonial New York*, p. 285.

[46]Olson, "Negro Slavery in New York," pp. 20-21, 20n; Goodfriend, "Burghers and Blacks," pp. 139-40; Janvier, "New York Slave-Traders," pp. 300-301; Innes, *New Amsterdam and Its People,* pp. 42-43; Riddell, "The Slave in Early New York," p. 60; Northrup, "Slavery in New York," p. 253; Davis, "Slavery in Colonial New York City," p. 42.

[47]*Anti-Slavery Standard*, 4 August 1860.

[48]Steven Deyle, "'By farr the most profitable trade': Slave Trading in British Colonial North America," *Slavery and Abolition*, vol. 10, no. 2 (September 1989), p. 109; James G. Lydon, "New York and the Slave Trade, 1700 to 1774," *William and Mary Quarterly*, vol. 35, no. 2 (April 1978), p. 381.

[49]Elizabeth Donnan, ed., *Documents Illustrative of the History of the Slave Trade to America*, vol. 3, *New England and the Middle Colonies* (Washington, DC: Carnegie Institution of Washington, 1932), pp. 462-512.

[50]Baird, *Chronicle of a Border Town*, p. 185; Robert C. Ritchie, "Samuel Burgess, Pirate," *Authority and Resistance in Early New York*, eds., William Pencak and Conrad Edick Wright, (New York: New-York Historical Society, 1988), pp. 127, 130; Singleton, *Dutch New York*, pp. 333, 338.

[51]Hartell, "Slavery on Long Island," p. 56.

[52]Cyrus H. Karraker, *Piracy was a Business* (Rindge, NH: Richard R. Smith Publisher, 1953), pp. 71, 80-81; Ritchie, "Samuel Burgess, Pirate," pp. 118, 119; Singleton, *Dutch New York*, p. 338.

[53]Karraker, *Piracy was a Business*, pp. 68-69, 70.

[54]Ellis, *Epic of New York City*, p. 286.

[55]Ernest A. McKay, *The Civil War and New York City* (Syracuse, NY: Syracuse Univ. Press, 1990), pp. 14-15.

[56]*Anti-Slavery Standard*, 7 July 1860.

[57]*Anti-Slavery Standard*, 4 August 1860.

[58]*Anti-Slavery Standard*, 7 July 1860.

[59]*Anti-Slavery Standard*, 7 July 1860.

New York Injustice

Denied by law a human personality, the slave could still reconstitute this personality out of the negativity the law bequeathed him, out of his potential to reach beyond the law and upset the social order. Should he break a law he would have no funds out of which to pay damages. In fact, if he had them, such funds would have been "prima facie" evidence of wrongdoing.[1]

New York developed a system of laws designed to subdue any impulse for freedom among its growing Black slave population. In the earliest Dutch period, custom dictated the racial hierarchy in the colony. Once the British took over in 1664, strict race codes were enacted that erased any racial ambiguity and firmly assigned Black New Yorkers to a legal sub-humanity which lasted well into the nineteenth century. The nature and character of race relations in early New York are eloquently evidenced in the severity of its oppressive slave code—indeed it was the harshest of all the English colonies. Conspiracy and sedition seemed to motivate the first wave of laws, but other laws appear to be motivated by a pure sadistic cruelty and Euro-savagery.[2]

Everyone participated in this wretched regime. The Quakers, the Presbyterians, the Catholics were all unified in their racist commandments. Incorporated into some of the laws was the phrase: "Slaves are the property of Christians." The Jews of New York, offended by this discrimination, successfully petitioned for inclusion. Subsequent oppressive anti-Black laws made it clear that slaves were the property of "Christians *and* Jews." Aside from legally designating Jews as *white* people, the law further defined slaves as being black-skinned, non-white, sub-human possessions. In fact, according to historian Thomas

J. Davis, "any amount of blackness was taken as *prima facie* evidence that a person was a slave."[3]

New York law did not recognize the possibility of a Black woman being raped. If the race of a child was in doubt, the law held that the child's status would be the same as the mother's. This law most assuredly staved off a flood of "free mulattos."[4]

Laws: New York Apartheid Laws

Below are some of the laws that existed in New York to control its Black population. Some were plainly malicious; others were designed to eliminate any means for Blacks to obtain any economic foundation. Even when these restrictive codes were repealed, the force of custom maintained the rigid code of exclusion from all forms of capital wealth.[5]

- More than three slaves congregating together was strictly forbidden on "penalty of being Whipt upon the Naked Back" up to 40 lashes. In an obvious pre-cursor to police policy of today, if Blacks were found congregating and they refused to submit to white authority, the police were to "fire upon them, kill or destroy them, if they cannot otherwise be taken."

- Blacks could not carry "guns, swords, clubs, staves, or any kind of weapon," on penalty of receiving ten lashes.

- Blacks were forbidden to ride horses, under penalty of 40 lashes.

- A law passed in 1692 decreed that any slave "playing or making any hooting or disorderly noise...or found in a publick house" on that day was to receive twenty lashes.

- "Negroes, Indians and Mulattoes" were prohibited from being on the street at night unless carrying a lantern.

- It was made an offense to buy from or sell to any slave without the consent of the master.

- "Free Negroes" in New York and New Jersey were not allowed to "enjoy, hold or possess any houses, lands, tenements or hereditaments within the colony."

- The sale of rum or other strong liquor to any "Negro, Indian, or Mulatto slave" was prohibited.

- A New York City ordinance provided that no more than twelve Blacks, in addition to the coffin-bearers and the gravedigger, could assemble at any funeral under penalty of public whipping. Another ordinance forbade the burial of Blacks after nightfall. Blacks were prevented by law from holding funerals after dark.

- Blacks were not permitted to pawn tools, apparel, or merchandise of any kind.

- It was decreed in 1740 that no Blacks were to sell vegetables or fruits in the city. Conviction meant a public whipping.

- Blacks guilty of drunkenness, cursing, being rude or stubborn "or talking impudently to any Christian" were to be whipped.

- Blacks were prevented by law from training dogs.

- Blacks from the country were forbidden to mingle with those from the city.[6]

Many of these harsh laws came into effect in 1702 under the regime of Queen Anne's cousin, Lord Cornbury, who imposed a criminal code which plainly did not apply to him. He embezzled funds from the public treasury to finance his all-night drunken parties and his purchases of ladies' garments, which he enjoyed wearing in public.[7] These laws were strengthened throughout the British rule, ever tightening the noose around the African.

With the approach of the 1776 American Revolution, the now 18,000 New York Blacks understood that even with British racism and British investment in the slave trade, life under the Americans would likely be worse. They allied with the British, who offered personal freedom and a measure of independence for those Blacks who were loyal to Britain during the war. According to scholars, "The choice of Loyalist permitted legal revenge against an American population that not only enslaved blacks but also terrorized them."[8]

When the Americans gained mastery over the land after the war, they wasted no time in imposing their own racist authority. They adopted and maintained the prevailing Black Codes and applied them with vigor. Far from conferring "freedom for all," one of the first New York legislative acts in 1781 was to encourage slave owners to deliver their Black slaves to the militia to defend the state.[9]

Laws: Torture and Punishment

Slaveholders in the North were exceedingly brutal. There is no such thing as a "kind master" and in New York *kindness* was against the law. The law actually assessed penalties for those given to "inappropriate and potentially disruptive kindness." Any master "forgiving, making up, compounding or compromising" was severely fined in New York. Blacks fought to overthrow the demonic system at every turn and sometimes they paid dearly.[10] Such revolts are remembered as "crimes" by white historians. But they fail to realize that Blacks, by definition, could commit no crimes in a society that did not acknowledge their humanity.

Nevertheless, revolts by Blacks were punished and the white man of New York seemed to relish the brutality that became common in the torture of his kidnapped Africans. Whipping, roasting, branding, hanging, deportation, and dungeoning were all used in New York's Black slave system. The cruelty became systematic and legalized and often applied with great fanfare.[11]

Most sizable New York communities employed "negro whippers" to beat their freedom-loving Africans. The method used in New York was to tie the Black victim to a cart and have him whipped a specified number of times at each street corner as he was dragged around the city. Cowardly whites often forced Blacks to inflict the torture upon their own people.[12]

New York City slavemasters would imprison Black slaves "indefinitely" in the Bridewell dungeon, which was used as a slave punishment center. Described as an "abode of wretchedness and misery," Bridewell held prisoners who were placed in irons in single cells seven by three and one-half feet and allowed neither to leave their cells nor to receive visitors, including their wives.[13] In 1842, English novelist Charles Dickens bitterly described the conditions at the prison, also known as The Tombs:

> Do men and women, against whom no crime is proved, lie here all night in perfect darkness, surrounded by the noisome vapours which encircle that flagging lamp you light us with, and breathing this filthy and offensive stench? Why, such indecent and disgusting dungeons as these cells would bring disgrace upon the most despotic empire in the world!....But if any one among them die in the interval, as one man did not long ago [t]hen he is half eaten by the rats in an hour's time... [14]

Deporting Blacks for "bad behavior" was another method of control often used in New York. More often the motive was to benefit from high prices for slaves in other regions of the New World. Hundreds of Blacks were ripped from their families and sent from New York in this way, along with legally "free" Blacks who could not prove their status.[15]

Laws: Persecution of Blacks in New York

The chart below presents a portion of the documented history of legal attacks against Blacks in New York. (The descriptions are from the sources noted.) The punishment meted out to suspected perpetrators has been appropriately described as "quite diabolic."[16]

Year	Accused	Charge	Sentence	Comment
1641	Manuel de Gerritt, a.k.a. the Giant	killing of a fellow-slave	The rope around his neck broke at the hanging. Superstitious whites pardoned him.	Six Blacks declared they had jointly committed the act, knowing that the execution of all six would be too costly. The court forced them to draw lots.
1646	Jan Creali	sodomy	Tied to a stake, and choked to death, his body burned.	Ten-year old victim was ordered tied to a stake, wood piled around him, and then released to be whipped.
1664	Negress Lysbet	arson	Ordered chained to a stake, strangled, and then burned.	Pardoned and returned to her master.
1677	Capt. William Palmer's slave	run away	50 lashes at the public whipping post.	
1679	Slaves Jacob, Claes and Black Barent	theft	Whipping and branding on face	Owner appealed and his slave Barent was branded on the back rather than on the face.
1682	Slave of Jacob Casperse	cut throats of 2 of owner's children and wounded a third.	Committed suicide; sheriff ordered body "hung as an example to others."	This slave may have hoped to find refuge among the Iroquois.
1684	A slave, of Harlem	suspected of arson which destroyed twelve cows	"hanging to a tree at the Little Hill by the common."	Mayor ordered the body hanged on a gibbet. But the magistrates, fearing the effect of such a sight upon their children, instead cut the body down and burned it.
1696	A slave named Prince	assault on Mayor Wm. Merritt	Stripped, tied to a cart and drawn through the city, 11 lashes at every corner.	Merritt was "assaulted on the face" while trying to disperse a group of "noisy Negroes."
1708	2 slaves — 1 Indian, 1 Black woman	killing of family of 7, of Long Island	One was hanged; other was burned at the stake in Jamaica.	They confessed, claiming revenge. "As the flames slowly consumed the Negro [woman], a horn filled with water was projected by means of a pole within reach of her mouth and tormentingly maneuvered before her 'as a terror to others.'"
1716	18-year-old Hannah	stealing cloth	Prosecuted and punished.	She stole the cloth "because she was almost naked and her mistress would give her no clothes."
1719	2 Black men	various "crimes"	Executed in Westchester county.	The men were appraised at £20 and payment was ordered, the slave owners reimbursed.
1732	"Negro Jack"	burning a barn and wheat	Burned alive.	Ulster County
1734	Slave of Mr. Vallet	assault of 15-year-old white girl	Sentenced to be burned alive.	The sentence was to serve as lesson to the many Blacks who witnessed it.

Year	Accused	Charge	Sentence	Comment
1735	Quacko	attempted rape	Sentenced to 39 lashes at Poughkeepsie, and an additional 48 at Rinebeck.	Dutchess County
1741	Tom	arson of a residence in NYC	Sentenced to be hanged.	He was twice reprieved in the hope that he would implicate others. Failing to do so, Tom was sent to his doom.
1756	nine Blacks	illegal assembly	Publicly whipped.	New York City
1772	Black slave	beat a white man to death	Hanged after short trial.	
1777	Jack, property of Dirck Hornbeck	"sought to ravish" a white woman		Despite the testimony of five whites in his behalf, was found guilty.
1788	Black women Nelly and Sarah, property of Vanderbilt	arson of the Vanderbilt home	Sentenced to be hanged.	Prosecution handled by Aaron Burr.
1793	Pompey, and two females, Bet and Dean	arson, property worth $250,000	Women were hanged; Pompey was executed before an immense gathering.	A last minute respite of six weeks disappointed the large audience assembled to witness their execution.
1793	Absalom	assault and theft	Public hanging	
1802	Slave of Capt. Fuller	mixed arsenic with the food served at a family meal	Executed	Dose was insufficient, for the Fullers recovered.
1808	Benjamin Than	murder	Public hanging	
1826	Ceasar	robbery	Public hanging	

Laws: Slave Owner Brutality

Most often, the slave owner himself inflicted the torture upon the Black slave. The New York Manumission Society reported in 1807 that it was frequently necessary to hospitalize slaves who had been victims of their owners' wrath.[17]

There are endless examples of abuse by the New York slave owner toward the defenseless African. The branding of Blacks was commonplace. In 1677 a New York City blacksmith, John Cooley, admitted beating his slave to death. He was acquitted.

In 1734 William Pettit killed his slave Jonathan, whom he kicked and beat "from head to foot." A year later, John Van Zandt's slave was lashed to death by his owner when he absented himself without permission. The Coroner's Jury, however, decided that death came not as the result of the whipping but by the "Visitations of God."[18]

The American era brought no change. In 1788 John Allen was indicted for torturing, flogging, and ultimately killing his slave. Allen was not punished. In 1794 L. Bertie punished a runaway Black woman, Julie, by having her breast marked with the name of her captor. In 1797 Gen. Thomas Machlin viciously beat to death an African named Michael.[19]

The early 1800s witnessed a Black man named Zeno forced to wear a heavy wooden collar around his neck. A New York City Frenchman named Beniwell was charged with whipping his four Africans "in a shocking manner" and "keeping them on an allowance of four potatoes apiece each day," when they failed to make 1,000 cigars each in a day. A Black child named Mary died of head wounds inflicted by her owner.[20]

In 1805 a Brooklyn slave owner punished his "young Negress" by hacking off a part of one ear and boring a hole in the other through which he suspended a large iron padlock. In that same year New York City slave owner Carl Hoffman abused 13-year-old James, who had run off wearing a brass collar on which Hoffman's name was engraved. Hoffman tied the boy's hands together, drew them up over his head by means of a rope attached to the wall, and fastened his feet to a staple on the floor, rubbing a mixture of salt and brandy over the open wounds. On a later occasion Hoffman, after beating the boy, forced James to swallow two table-spoonfuls of salt to stimulate thirst, then confined him in a room for two days without food or drink. He was fined $250 and posted a $2000 bond as a guarantee of his future behavior. But Hoffman continued his behavior and was again indicted. Rather than stand trial he chose to manumit the boy.[21]

Laws: **New York's Black Death Penalty**

New Yorkers did not hesitate to apply the death penalty to Blacks for any behavior they deemed inappropriate. Even the owners of the condemned Africans could enjoy the morbid festivities. They were compensated in cash for the appraised value of their "doomed Negro."[22] Crimes for which Blacks received the death penalty included:

- running away
- assault on their Master or Mistress
- burning of houses, outhouses or barns
- burning of Corn or hay, or the killing of Cattle
- murder or attempt to murder
- rape or attempt to rape a freewoman, but not the rape of a female slave
- traveling alone forty miles above the city of Albany[23]

More Blacks were put to death during the colonial period in New York than in any other northern colony. New Jersey was a close second. Atrocities, such as the posting of severed heads on wooden stakes, were not uncommon. The smell of Blacks being burned alive seemed to delight early white New Yorkers. The town would gather for the event with much anticipation.[24] An early observer describes one such affair:

> The criminal was chained to a stake with light wood thrown around him. If the torture was to be prolonged then green wood was used, and the executioner supplied him with water to quench his thirst, by means of a cow-horn fastened to the end of a pole.

The same writer explained that, "It was not unusual to hang up negroes in a wooden frame so that they might die of starvation and their carcasses be devoured by birds of prey."[25]

Laws: New York Medieval

Other forms of debasement meted out to slaves and recorded in the state's archives are the following:

- wearing of brass collars
- branding with a hot iron on the forehead or cheek
- breaking on the wheel (a horrifyingly slow process of breaking a victim's bones one at a time)
- maiming
- castration
- pilloring (locked in a wooden rack for a length of time)
- wrenching (forcibly twisting the body)
- riding a wooden horse (The wooden horse was shaped like a carpenter's sawhorse and the punishment consisted of straddling the crossbar for hours with weights of up to fifty pounds attached to each leg.)[26]

Blacks who were thought to be intoxicated were dunked in the harbor or forced to swallow "a plentiful dose" of salt water and lamp oil.[27] Even suicide would not deprive the white man of his thirst for Black suffering. In 1697 a courageous Black man justly killed a white man and received the death sentence. He took his own life before the execution but officials ordered that punishment be inflicted on his dead body. The lifeless remains of this official New York lynching also had a function: "The swaying corpses of such Negroes often remained suspended for several days after the execution to terrorize slaves into good behaviour."[28]

Notes

[1]Carl Nordstrom, "The New York Slave Code," *Afro-Americans in New York Life and History*, vol. 4, no. 1 (January 1980), p. 12.

[2]Douglas Greenberg, "Patterns of Criminal Prosecution in Eighteenth-Century New

notes, continued

York," *New York History*, vol. 56, no. 2 (April 1975), pp. 139, 140; Nordstrom, "The New York Slave Code," pp. 7-11, 16; A. Judd Northrup, "Slavery in New York," *State Library Bulletin*, History No. 4 (May 1900), p. 255; Richard Shannon Moss, *Slavery on Long Island: A Study in Local Institutional and Early African-American Communal Life* (1993), p. 18; Edwin Olson, "The Slave Code in Colonial New York," *Journal of Negro History*, vol. 29, no. 2 (April 1944), p. 147; Edwin Vernon Morgan, "Slavery in New York, with Special Reference to New York City," *Slavery in the States: Selected Essays* (New York: Negro Universities Press, 1969), pp. 12-13; Edwin Olson, "Negro Slavery in New York, 1626-1827" (Ph.D. thesis, New York Univ., 1938), p. 87; Roi Ottley and William J. Weatherby, eds., *The Negro in New York: An Informal Social History* (Dobbs Ferry, NY: Oceana Publications, 1967), p. 24; Thomas J. Davis, "The New York Slave Conspiracy of 1741 As Black Protest," *Journal of Negro History*, vol. 56, no. 1 (1971), p. 38[22].

[3]*The Colonial Laws of New York from the Year 1664 to the Revolution*, vol. 1 (Albany, 1894), pp. 519-20; Thomas Joseph Davis, "Slavery in Colonial New York City" (Ph.D. diss., Columbia Univ., 1974), pp. 74, 78; Olson, "Negro Slavery in New York," p. 82; *The Colonial Laws of New York from the Year 1664 to the Revolution*, vol. 2 (Albany, 1894), pp. 681, 683; Nordstrom, "The New York Slave Code," p. 12; Kenneth Jackson, ed., *Encyclopedia of New York City* (Yale Univ. Press, 1995), p. 1076.

[4]Linda Grant De Pauw, *Four Traditions: Women of New York During the American Revolution* (Albany: N.Y. State American Revolution Bicentennial Commission, 1974), p. 8; Moss, *Slavery on Long Island*, p. 20.

[5]Morgan, "Slavery in New York," pp. 7-8, 10, 13-16; *Colonial Laws of New York*, vol. 2, pp. 679-87; Michael Kammen, *Colonial New York–A History* (New York: Charles Scribner's Sons, 1975), p. 283; Nordstrom, "The New York Slave Code," pp. 9-11, 14, 16, 19; Leo H. Hirsch, Jr., "The Negro and New York, 1783-1865," *Journal of Negro History*, vol. 16, no. 4, (October 1931), p. 397; Greenberg, "Patterns of Criminal Prosecution," pp. 139, 140, 144; David M. Ellis et al., *A Short History of New York State* (Ithaca, NY: Cornell Univ. Press in cooperation with the N. Y. State Historical Association, 1957), p. 62; Anne Hartell, "Slavery on Long Island," *Nassau County Historical Journal*, vol. 6, no. 2 (fall 1943), p. 62; Peter Ross, *A History of Long Island: From its Earliest Settlement to the Present Time*, vol. 1 (New York: Lewis, 1902), pp. 119-20.

[6]William Renwick Riddell, "The Slave in Early New York," *Journal of Negro History*, vol. 13, no. 1 (January 1928), p. 68; Ottley and Weatherby, *The Negro in New York*, pp. xvii, 21-22, 26; Olson, "Negro Slavery in New York," pp. 87-89; Nordstrom, "The New York Slave Code," pp. 10-11, 12; Davis, "Slavery in Colonial New York City," p. 84; Olson, "The Slave Code in Colonial New York," pp. 153, 155; Greenberg, "Patterns of Criminal Prosecution," p. 139; *The Colonial Laws of New York*, vol. 1, pp. 519, 761-62, 764; *Colonial Laws of New York*, vol. 2, pp. 679-80; Northrup, "Slavery in New York," pp. 265, 270; Hirsch, "The Negro and New York, " p. 384; Lorman Ratner, *Powder Keg: Northern Opposition to the Antislavery Movement, 1831-1840* (New York: Basic Books, 1968), pp. 7, 8; Morgan, "Slavery in New York," p. 22; Jackson, *Encyclopedia of New York City*, p. 1076; Hartell, "Slavery on Long Island," pp. 62, 64.

[7]Ottley and Weatherby, *The Negro in New York*, p. 21.

[8]Paul A. Gilje and William Pencak, eds., *New York in the Age of the Constitution, 1775-*

notes, continued

1800 (Cranbury, NJ: Associated Univ. Presses, 1992), pp. 22, 23-24.

[9]Nordstrom, "The New York Slave Code," pp. 17, 18; Northrup, "Slavery in New York," p. 287; Ottley and Weatherby, *The Negro in New York*, p. 36.

[10]Gary Kriss, "When Westchester Had Slaves: A Catalogue of Unseen Faces," *New York Times*, 19 October 1997, sec. 14, p. 22; Nordstrom, "The New York Slave Code," p. 16; Davis, "The New York Slave Conspiracy," p. 45[29].

[11]Olson, "The Slave Code in Colonial New York," pp. 162-64; Davis, "Slavery in Colonial New York City," pp. 78-79; Leopold S. Launitz-Schurer, Jr., "Slave Resistance in Colonial New York: An Interpretation of Daniel Horsmanden's New York Conspiracy," *Phylon*, vol. 41, no. 2 (June 1980), pp. 138-39; Lawrence B. Goodheart, "'The Chronicles of Kidnapping in New York': Resistance to the Fugitive Slave Law, 1834-1835," *Afro-Americans in New York Life and History*, vol. 8, no. 1 (January 1984), p. 11.

[12]Ottley and Weatherby, *The Negro in New York*, p. 21; Olson, "Negro Slavery in New York," pp. 102, 132; Olson, "The Slave Code in Colonial New York," p. 163; Davis, "Slavery in Colonial New York City," pp. 93-94.

[13]Olson, "The Slave Code in Colonial New York," pp. 164-65; Olson, "Negro Slavery in New York," pp. 103, 104; Goodheart, "'The Chronicles of Kidnapping'," pp. 11-12.

[14]Charles Dickens, *American Notes* (1842; reprint, New York: St. Martin's Press, 1985), p. 83.

[15]Olson, "Negro Slavery in New York," pp. 145, 146; Edwin Olson, "Social Aspects of the Slave in New York," *Journal of Negro History*, vol. 26, no. 1 (January 1941), pp. 74-76; Davis, "Slavery in Colonial New York City," pp. 209, 215.

[16]Olson, "Negro Slavery in New York," pp. 26-27, 28, 96, 97, 98-99, 100-101, 132; Ottley and Weatherby, *The Negro in New York*, pp. 7-8, 22-23; Henry H. Kessler and Eugene Rachlis, *Peter Stuyvesant and His New York* (New York: Random House, 1959), p. 21; Davis, "Slavery in Colonial New York City," pp. 57, 58, 93-94; Thomas E. Burke, Jr., *Mohawk Frontier: The Dutch Community of Schenectady, New York, 1661-1710* (Ithaca, NY: Cornell Univ. Press, 1991), p. 132; Greenberg, "Patterns of Criminal Prosecution," pp. 141n, 146; Morgan, "Slavery in New York," pp. 9-10; Hartell, "Slavery on Long Island," pp. 63-64; Olson, "The Slave Code in Colonial New York," pp. 153, 162; Thomas J. Davis, "These Enemies of Their Own Household: A Note on the Troublesome Slave Population in Eighteenth-Century New York City," *Journal of the Afro-American Historical and Genealogical Society*, vol. 5 (1984), p. 138; Charles W. Baird, *Chronicle of a Border Town: History of Rye, Westchester County, New York, 1660-1870* (New York, 1871; reprint, Harrison, NY: Harbor Hill Books, 1974), p. 184; A. J. Williams-Myers, "The African Presence in the Mid-Hudson Valley Before 1800: A Preliminary Historiographical Sketch," *Afro-Americans in New York Life and History*, vol. 8, no. 1 (January 1984), p. 33; Davis, "The New York Slave Conspiracy," p. 35n[19n]. Arson was a common "crime" of slaves. See Herbert Aptheker, *American Negro Slave Revolts* (New York, 1943), 144-49.

[17]Olson, "Negro Slavery in New York," p. 144.

[18]Olson, "Negro Slavery in New York," pp. 45, 131, 144-45; Olson, "Social Aspects of the Slave in New York," p. 74; Davis, "Slavery in Colonial New York City," p. 177.

[19]Hartell, "Slavery on Long Island," pp. 64-65; Olson, "Negro Slavery in New York," pp. 131, 145.

notes, continued

[20]Olson, "Negro Slavery in New York," pp. 132, 144; Hartell, "Slavery on Long Island,"p. 65.

[21]Olson, "Negro Slavery in New York," pp. 132, 143-44.

[22]Olson, "The Slave Code in Colonial New York," p. 150; Ottley and Weatherby, *The Negro in New York*, p. 20n; Nordstrom, "The New York Slave Code," p. 13.

[23]Olson, "Negro Slavery in New York," p. 84; Nordstrom, "The New York Slave Code," p. 13; Olson, "The Slave Code in Colonial New York," p. 149; Kammen, *Colonial New York*, p. 284; Davis, "Slavery in Colonial New York City," p. 77.

[24]Gilje and Pencak,*New York in the Age of the Constitution*, pp. 23-24; Riddell, "The Slave in Early New York," p. 69; Davis, "Slavery in Colonial New York City," pp. 78-79, 94.

[25]Hartell, "Slavery on Long Island," p. 65.

[26]Olson, "The Slave Code in Colonial New York," p. 163; Davis, "Slavery in Colonial New York City," pp. 78-79; Olson, "Negro Slavery in New York," pp. 131-32, 143-45; Kammen, *Colonial New York*, pp. 58, 284; Edward Robb Ellis, *The Epic of New York City* (New York: Coward-McCann, 1966), pp. 113-14; Kessler and Rachlis, *Peter Stuyvesant*, p. 18; Henri Van der Zee, *A Sweet and Alien Land: The Story of Dutch New York* (New York: Viking Press, 1978), p. 100; Nordstrom, "The New York Slave Code," p. 21.

[27]Edgar J. McManus, *Black Bondage in the North* (Syracuse, NY: Syracuse Univ. Press, 1973), p. 82.

[28]Davis, "Slavery in Colonial New York City," p. 94; Olson, "The Slave Code in Colonial New York," p. 162.

Surviving Under New York Slavery

Once the British overthrew the Dutch regime in 1664, they began to formalize their relationship with the growing African population. This state of racial affairs continued unabated under the reign of the new Americans more than a century later.

Surviving: New York Under Garbage

The living conditions and maltreatment faced by the Africans were intolerably primitive and rudely medieval. The Europeans simply threw their garbage into the street among the dead animals and other refuse, and African slaves were forced to clear it.[1] More than a half-century from the American Revolution, Charles Dickens seemed to be holding his nose as he described his buggy ride down the Great White Way:

> Take care of the pigs. Two portly sows are trotting up behind this carriage, and a select party of half-a-dozen gentlemen hogs have just now turned the corner. Here is a solitary swine....He is in every respect a republican pig, going wherever he pleases, and mingling with the best society, on an equal, if not superior footing, for every one makes way when he appears, and the haughtiest give him the wall, if he prefer it....They are the city scavengers, these pigs. Ugly brutes they are.[2]

The herds of pigs were, in fact, the first New York street cleaners, amidst extreme, disease-ridden squalor. It has been said that the initiation of garbage collection "saved more lives in the crowded tenements than a squad of doctors."[3]

It is entirely appropriate that the pig was employed in this manner in New York as it was in Europe. Tracing back the origin of the name *York*, one would find that its root is in the early English term meaning "wild-boar place."[4]

Surviving: **The Black Uprising of 1712**

The legal structure tightened its noose around the Black slave and resentment smoldered in New York. The resulting powder keg soon ignited into open rebellion.

The Black Uprising of 1712 stands as one of the greatest acts of courage by the Africans of early New York. Despite overwhelming oppression intended to extinguish all hope of freedom in the Black man and woman, they yet planned an uprising designed to slaughter their white enemies and gain justice in their lifetimes.

On the night of April 6, 1712, a fire alarm was sounded in the center of the town. As the whites converged on the scene thirty Black men descended upon them, shooting, slashing and hacking with guns, knives and hatchets. The Black rebels were able only to kill nine and wound six whites before the militia chased them into the countryside. The next morning, when they were found in their forest hiding place, six had committed suicide, one man killing his wife and himself. The rest were captured and "tried."[5]

"Then, as with one diseased mind," wrote historian Edward Robb Ellis, "the white colonists settled down to the punishment of the colored revolutionaries." Twenty-one Black freedom fighters

FOR SALE,
A young Black Girl, fix years old, ftout and rugged. Any perfon wifhing to purchafe can apply to the fubfcriber, five miles weft of the yellow Meeting Houfe, in Cambridge. JOSHUA BROWNELL.

Figure 11 - *Farmer's Register*, August 5, 1806

were arrested, tried, convicted, tortured and murdered. One was a pregnant woman carrying a valuable slave, so her sentence was suspended. Another woman, however, was hanged.[6]

- A Black hero, named Robin, who had stabbed his master in the back, "was suspended alive in chains without food or water until he expired after days of unspeakable anguish."

- Two Blacks were burned alive over a slow fire. "The acrid odor of singed flesh irritated the nostrils of spectators during the eight to ten hours the Negroes suffered."

- Another Black man, who had wounded a constable, was stripped to the waist, tied to the end of a cart in front of City Hall, dragged through lower Manhattan, and lashed bloodily ten times at every street corner.

- One Black man was broken on the wheel:

His eyeballs bulging in terror, he was bound, face up, on a large cartwheel set on a platform. Then the wheel was raised to an inclined position so that every onlooker could have a clear view. After that, the public executioner picked up a sledgehammer, raised it high above his head, and slammed it down on one bound arm. Slowly, deliberately, painstakingly, the hammer rose and fell, rose and fell, blow after thudding blow, smashing to pulp the arms and legs of the shrieking black man. Now the attack was directed to the trembling torso until one murderous whack over the heart killed the condemned.[7]

There were other casualties. Some whites blamed the rebellion on the indoctrination that some slaves were receiving at the Trinity Church school conducted by Elias Neau. They physically assailed him until it was shown that none of the conspirators attended his school. Neau used this vindication to promote his program, suggesting that conversion and proper instruction made Blacks better slaves.[8]

The result of the uprising among the petrified whites was to pass legislation for still more proto-Nazi New York laws. "An Act for Preventing, Suppressing and Punishing the Conspiracy and Insurrection of Negroes and other Slaves," passed December 10, 1712, and a "Law for Regulating Negro and Indian Slaves in the Night Time" passed in March of 1713.[9]

To be Sold,

A LIKELY Young Negro Wench, about 24 years old, with a male child about 2 years old ; the Wench is fit for either town or country.   Enquire of the Printer.
Albany. Auguft 4, 1783.   62—

R AN-AWAY from the Subfcriber, on the Night of the 15th inft. a NEGRO MAN named Quom, fhort ftature, well fet, had on a brown Cloth Coat with green Bafket Buttons, Linen under Cloths, about 20 years old, fpeaks low Dutch and Englifh,—Alfo, an apprentice Lad, named Herculus Lent, about 17 years old, had on a brown Worfted Coat, a white Caftor Hatt,—each of them wore a pair of large Oval carved block-tin Buckles. Whoever fecures the NEGRO, and gives word to Theodorou's V. W. Graham, Efq ; in Albany, fhall there receive TEN DOLLARS Reward, and all reafonable charges, or on notice given to the Subfcriber, the Reward and charges will be paid by   THOMAS STORM.
Hopewell, Dutchefs County, July 28, 1783

Ten Dollars Reward.

R AN-AWAY from the Subfcriber, living in Albany, on the 25th of July, a black NE-GRO FELLOW named TOM ; 22 years old, about 5 Feet eight Inches high, has a fcar below one of his eyes, his knees bent inwardly,—he fpeaks good Dutch and Englifh : Had on when he went off, a Tow fhirt and Overalk, an old wool Hatt. Whoever takes up faid Rnusway and confines him in any Goal, and informs the Subfcriber, fo that he may get him again, fhall receive the above reward, with all reafonable charges, and many thanks, from   PETER GANSEVORT.
Albany, Auguft 4, 1783.

Figure 12 - *New York Gazette*, August 4, 1783

Surviving: White Murder Orgy of 1741

It is generally believed that the infamous Witch Trials of Salem, Massachusetts, is a uniquely ghoulish event in American history. Twenty teenaged white girls were executed in 1692 after having been "found guilty" of casting spells upon the populace. A more frightening story of racism, mass murder and "witchcraft" unfolded in 1741 New York City, and it is largely forgotten in the history books of America. Indeed, it is considered to be "the most tragic event of New York Colonial history."[10]

The satanic assault on innocent New York Blacks is known as the White Murder Orgy of 1741. When the fury subsided, 154 Blacks had been cast into the dungeon, 14 of them burned alive, 18 hanged, 2 gibbeted (hanged in chains while alive), and 71 transported from the colony. Twenty whites who were thought to be collaborating with the Blacks were also imprisoned but only four were executed.[11]

The surviving story of the White Murder Orgy of 1741 is entirely a creation of white folks. Judge Daniel Horsmanden, who solemnly orchestrated the "trial" of the Black victims, is the primary source for the "facts" surrounding the events of that year.[12] The story goes as follows:

In March of 1741, an African with the given name of "Quack" came to visit his wife, who was held in captivity by Lieutenant Governor Clarke. Clarke had earlier forbidden Quack from seeing his wife and the African was refused entry.

It was claimed that an angry and vindictive Quack threatened to burn down the governor's house, and all of Fort George, which was then at the foot of Broadway. Within a few days, Quack, proving to be a man of his word, burned the buildings to the ground. He "confessed" to setting the blaze, and he himself was publicly burned to death over a slow fire.[13]

The seething resentment among Blacks now intensified. Whites knew, as many know today, that given the opportunity, Blacks would change their condition and confront their oppressors with violence if necessary. The paranoia that constantly embraced Caucasian New Yorkers was palpable and caused them to suspect even the most doting Uncle Toms. Blacks were immediately suspected when several fires of dubious origin broke out. A reward of £100 and a full pardon had been offered to anyone who could give information concerning the supposed "negro plot." Mary Burton was a 16-year-old white indentured servant who had been accused of thievery. Seeing an opportunity for her own escape she began to weave a fantastic tale of intrigue and terror in which, she claimed, Blacks planned to destroy the city and make *her white master* king. The Black brutes would then ravish the white women, who would become their slaves. No proof was necessary. No supporting testimony or evidence was supplied or asked for by piqued whites, who immediately began their barbarous orgy with the arrests of scores of Blacks and an assortment of disaffected whites.[14]

TEN DOLLARS REWARD.

RAN away from the subscriber, living at Flatbush, on Long-Island, a black man named DICK, five feet nine inches high, aged 28 years, speaks Dutch, of a smiling countenance, not so black as negroes in common are; had on when he went away a brown great coat and brown under coat, corduroy vest and homespun trowsers, wears his hair tied, his shoes on the soals full of nails. Whoever will apprehend said negro, or secure him in any goal, so that his master shall receive him again, will be paid the above reward and all reasonable charges. HENRY HAVENS.

N. B. Masters of vessels and others are forbid carrying off said Negro, or harbor him at their Peril.

Figure 13 - *The Diary*, March 11, 1784

By this time in 1741, 2,000 of New York's 12,000 residents were Black slaves and that provoked many complaints about their "great numbers" having "too great liberties." "[T]hey whetted their knives...and some [Blacks] said their knives were sharp enough to cut off a white man's head," claimed one observer. Some even said that a Black captive named Caesar had obtained "seven or eight guns, three pistols and four swords."[15]

Horsmanden himself was one of the main purveyors of the race paranoia that set the tone for the pogrom:

> [T]his city and province [might] be warned to keep themselves upon a strict guard against *these enemies of their own household*, since we know what they are capable of; for it was notorious, that those among them, who had the kindest masters, who fared best, and had the most liberty, nay, that those in whom their masters placed the greatest confidence, insomuch, that they would even have put their own swords into their hands, in the expectation of being defended by them...did nevertheless turn out the greatest villains.[16]

New York's Judicial Witchcraft

> *We shall never be quite safe, till that wicked race are under more restraint, or their number greatly reduced within this city.*   —*Prosecutor*[17]

The New York White Murder Orgy "trials" began in the summer of 1741 and continued for more than a year. The bizarre ritual that preceded the orgy of Black sacrifices was a showpiece of colonial New York justice:

- The Blacks were denied legal counsel, as the entire bar of the city offered its services to the prosecution.

- The central theme of the prosecution's case was simply that the "Negro plot" was the result of a Spanish and Catholic endeavor to overwhelm New York.

- Only confession of guilt could save an accused person from the gallows; and more than 70 who "confessed" were exiled to the West Indies.[18]

A white man named Arthur Price, in jail for stealing, now became a willing informer. As a result of his having pretended to receive "confessions" of some "co-conspirators," even more Blacks were imprisoned. Price's "extraordinary" ability to obtain incriminating statements delighted the prosecution. "No confession was a success unless it implicated someone not yet suspected," wrote historian Edwin Olson.[19]

"The hysteria and trials finally ended when Mary Burton began to name prominent, respectable citizens and thereby lost all her credibility. She received her hundred-pound reward nonetheless and promptly disappeared from the province."[20]

Torture of the Black Victims

Numerous salivating whites gathered for the executions. Moreover, a proud inquisitor was delighted to have "rid this country of some of the vilest creatures in it." Indeed, the prosecutions cut the city's population of adult male slaves by about one-seventh. More would have died had it not been for a heat wave which was thought might breed an epidemic in the overcrowded jail. Pardons were granted to 44 imprisoned Blacks on condition that they be transported from the colony.[21]

It was noticed that a white man's body, after hanging for three weeks on the gibbet, had turned black and that his hair seemed kinky, whereas the face of the Black man, Caesar, whose body swung nearby, had turned whitish. The spectacle attracted curious crowds from near and far.[22]

Surviving: The Black Holocaust: Statewide

Among the whites of the New York hinterlands, a climate of fear and hate prevailed. An open and bloody Black rebellion was considered imminent at all times. For this reason the census data are filled with inaccuracies. Census recorders obscured population data in areas where Blacks were in great numbers. Historian A. J. Williams-Myers wrote that, "Wherever there were large concentrations of Africans these [census] figures were never published. This was particularly true for the period after the early slave revolts..."[23] Nonetheless, evidence of New York's brutal slave regime exists for every region.

Long Island: Early on, the Indian population was swiftly reduced by half, the remainder to dependent status, by the European onslaught. Until the mid-1750s, Long Islanders held more enslaved Africans than colonists in the New England or mid-Atlantic colonies. The plantations on the peninsula were needed to supply Manhattan with foodstuffs, so Black slavery became essential. The African female population was used primarily as domestics, with African males employed on farms as day laborers. One of their main functions was to pound Indian corn on stone with fifty-pound blocks. This became known as "niggering corn."[24]

Long Islanders did not give up their slave property easily. The members of the state Assembly representing Long Island voted as a bloc against the *Gradual Emancipation Act* and related legislation.[25]

Westchester County: When whites first settled here they brought captive Africans as slaves. A 1698 census shows 146 Africans in Westchester, 13.7 percent of the population. In 1739, the town of Rye in Westchester County chose Thomas Rickey to be the public whipper. In 1747 Samuel Bumpos was chosen to the same "office." By 1771, Westchester had 3,137 Blacks, surpassing the number in Manhattan. It was considered common for households to have one or two captive slaves, but at least one wealthy household held 23.

According to an area historian, "the free blacks in Westchester often lived in conditions as wretched as slaves."

When slavery was "abolished" in 1827, "vestiges continued until the Civil War."[26]

Rochester: According to the Rev. Orlo J. Price, "History is strangely silent about the slaves of our early settlers." But Colonel Nathaniel Rochester, founder of the city, left Hagerstown, Maryland, with ten enslaved Black Africans. It is claimed that he then "freed" them. The Rochester Historical Society wrote: "It is not likely that the first white settler on the site of what is now Rochester—Ebenezer Allan, generally known as Indian Allan—had any strong bias against the enslavement of the Negro race."[27]

Albany: Albany (Fort Orange) was established on the "Far frontier" in the early 17th century, but failed to attract white settlers because of frontier conditions. This made those who did settle dependent upon slave labor. But many Africans escaped and joined the friendly Indian tribes. In 1705 a law was passed to try to abate this problem, prohibiting Africans from traveling 40 miles north of Saratoga, present-day Schuylerville. Violation meant the death penalty.[28]

In 1793 three courageous Africans fought back. Carrying coals in a shoe, one Black insurgent set fire to Albany. All three freedom fighters, including two Black women, were executed in front of a massive crowd of bloodthirsty Europeans.[29]

Schenectady: The Indians called the Albany area *Schenectadea*, "the place you reach by traveling through pine woods." At least one sixth of Schenectady residents held African slaves after 1661, and by 1690 enslaved Blacks had become "an important factor in Schenectady's demography, economy, and culture." In 1761 thirteen Africans were arrested after they had been "overheard in a tavern planning to burn and loot the town."[30]

To be SOLD,

A Healthy Negro Wench, of about 12 or 13 years of age, has had the small pox, and is very handy about the house.—For further particulars apply to the Printer.

Figure 13 - *Weekly Museum*, April 5, 1794.

Surviving: **"Anti-Slavery" – So-called**

In January of 1785 several whites organized the New York Manumission Society. To most white historians, that act alone is proof of the "true nature" of the New York heart in the matter of chattel slavery. But curiously, "[t]he society neither expected nor attempted to effect any sudden alteration in the laws relating to slavery." Many prominent slaveholding New Yorkers participated in the charade, including John Jay and Alexander Hamilton. According to the 1790 census, 27 of the 120 members in the Society were slave owners. Governor George Clinton owned eight slaves, Chief Justice Richard Morris six, and Aaron Burr five. John Jay, the president of the Manumission Society, also owned five slaves. For a quarter of a century, the Society's own members defeated every motion that they *manumit their own slaves.* In fact, Alexander Hamilton, who made the motion, never freed his.[31]

It is suggested, and probably with great veracity, that the Manumission Society was motivated by the desire of these wealthy Federalists to make partisan voters of their own freed slaves. After all, "in his voting, as well as in his talk and dress, the Negro should follow the example of his former master."[32]

Despite their inability to be true to their own stated purpose, the Society members did intervene in many cases of legal abuse of Black New Yorkers, slave and "free." From 1785 to 1825, they handled 3,000 such cases involving 6,000 Blacks, of which probably 1,500 were settled in the Blacks' favor. The Society dismantled shortly after the statewide "abolition" was achieved in 1817. Many former Society members then chose to promote colonization of "freed" slaves—that is, the deportation and resettlement of the unwanted Africans in Africa. With this they were marginally more successful. In March 1820 the *Elizabeth* sailed from New York City for Africa with 86 Blacks, of whom 40 were from the State of New York. During the next forty years they took 10,586 Blacks to Africa.[33]

Surviving: **The End of Legal Slavery in New York**

After rejecting abolition several times, the state legislature passed the New York Manumission Act of 1799. It achieved the *gradual* abolition of slavery and provided that all male children and teens would have to remain enslaved until 28 years of age and females until they were 25.

The actual legal end came with no fanfare on the fourth of July, 1827. The *New York Evening Post* did not even mention the event. Travelers, however, could still bring African captives into New York for not more than nine months, but as late as 1850 there was at least one "aged" enslaved African in Putnam County.[34]

Notes

[1] Morton Wagman, "Corporate Slavery in New Netherland," *Journal of Negro History*, vol. 65, no. 1 (winter 1980), p. 37.

[2] Charles Dickens, *American Notes* (1842; reprint, New York: St. Martin's Press, 1985), pp. 77-78.

[3] Jacob A. Riis, *A Ten Years' War: An Account of the Battle with the Slum in New York* (Boston & New York: Houghton, Mifflin, 1900), pp. 172-75.

[4] George R. Stewart, *Names On the Land: A Historical Account of Place-Naming in the United States* (Boston: Houghton Mifflin, 1967), p. 79.

[5] Roi Ottley and William J. Weatherby, eds., *The Negro in New York: An Informal Social History* (Dobbs Ferry, NY: Oceana Publications, 1967), p. 23; Thomas J. Davis, "These Enemies of Their Own Household: A Note on the Troublesome Slave Population in Eighteenth-Century New York City," *Journal of the Afro-American Historical and Genealogical Society*, vol. 5 (1984), pp. 137-38; Leopold S. Launitz-Schurer, Jr., "Slave Resistance in Colonial New York: An Interpretation of Daniel Horsmanden's New York Conspiracy," *Phylon*, vol. 41, no. 2 (June 1980), p. 140; Thomas Joseph Davis, "Slavery in Colonial New York City" (Ph.D. diss., Columbia Univ., 1974), pp. 96, 106.

[6] Edward Robb Ellis, *The Epic of New York City* (New York: Coward-McCann, 1966), pp. 113-14; Davis, "Slavery in Colonial New York City," p. 105; William Renwick Riddell, "The Slave in Early New York," *Journal of Negro History*, vol. 13, no. 1 (January 1928), p. 71.

[7] Ellis, *Epic of New York City*, pp. 113-14.

[8] Davis, "Slavery in Colonial New York City," pp. 108-109.

[9] Edwin Vernon Morgan, "Slavery in New York, with Special Reference to New York City," *Slavery in the States: Selected Essays* (New York: Negro Universities Press, 1969), p. 13; Davis, "Slavery in Colonial New York City," p. 109.

[10] Morgan, "Slavery in New York," pp. 16-17; The hysteria surrounding the Salem Witch Trials also had racial overtones. Some of the "witches" blamed their "spells" on Tituba, a West Indian-born Black woman whose mastery of the healing arts spooked

notes, continued

white people, whose medical expertise amounted to draining blood from sick people. Charles E. Corwin, "Efforts of the Dutch Colonial Pastors for the Conversion of the Negroes," *Journal of the Presbyterian Historical Society*, vol. 12, no. 7, (April 1927), p. 431.

[11]Morgan, "Slavery in New York," pp. 17-18.

[12]Launitz-Schurer, "Slave Resistance in Colonial New York," pp. 139-40.

[13]Davis, "These Enemies of Their Own Household," p. 136; Launitz-Schurer, "Slave Resistance in Colonial New York," p. 137; Thomas J. Davis, "The New York Slave Conspiracy of 1741 As Black Protest," *Journal of Negro History*, vol. 56, no. 1 (1971), p. 35[19].

[14]Launitz-Schurer, "Slave Resistance in Colonial New York," pp. 137-38; Davis, "Slavery in Colonial New York City," p. 128; Davis, "The New York Slave Conspiracy," pp. 35[19], 36[20]; Michael Kammen, *Colonial New York–A History* (New York: Charles Scribner's Sons, 1975), p. 285; Morgan, "Slavery in New York," p. 17.

[15]Davis, "These Enemies of Their Own Household," p. 133; Davis, "The New York Slave Conspiracy," pp. 35[19], 45[29]; Davis, "Slavery in Colonial New York City," p. 127.

[16]Davis, "The New York Slave Conspiracy," p. 39[23]; Davis, "Slavery in Colonial New York City," pp. 127-28.

[17]Davis, "These Enemies of Their Own Household," p. 133.

[18]Edwin Olson, "Negro Slavery in New York, 1626-1827" (Ph.D. thesis, New York Univ., 1938), pp. 118, 123; Launitz-Schurer, "Slave Resistance in Colonial New York," pp. 138-39; Kammen, *Colonial New York*, p. 285.

[19]Olson, "Negro Slavery in New York," pp. 117, 119.

[20]Kammen, *Colonial New York*, p. 285.

[21]Launitz-Schurer, "Slave Resistance in Colonial New York," pp. 138-39; Riddell, "The Slave in Early New York," p. 71; Davis, "The New York Slave Conspiracy," p. 34 [18]; Olson, "Negro Slavery in New York," pp. 121, 123; Davis, "These Enemies of Their Own Household," p. 139.

[22]Olson, "Negro Slavery in New York," p. 120.

[23]A. J. Williams-Myers, "The African Presence in the Mid-Hudson Valley Before 1800: A Preliminary Historiographical Sketch," *Afro-Americans in New York Life and History*, vol. 8, no. 1 (January 1984), p. 33.

[24]Richard Shannon Moss, *Slavery on Long Island: A Study in Local Institutional and Early African-American Communal Life*, (1993), pp. xi, xiii-xiv, 14, 23, 24; Mario Charles and Sandra Roff, "Black Images from the Past: Attitudes Presented in the *Long Island Star* and the *New York Evening Post* in the Early 1820s," *Afro-Americans in New York Life and History*, vol. 18, no. 2 (July 1994), p. 8; Olson, "Negro Slavery in New York," p. 55.

[25]Moss, *Slavery on Long Island*, p. xv.

[26] Charles W. Baird, *Chronicle of a Border Town: History of Rye, Westchester County, New York, 1660-1870* (New York, 1871; reprint, Harrison, NY: Harbor Hill Books, 1974), p. 183; Gary Kriss, "When Westchester Had Slaves: A Catalogue of Unseen Faces," *New York Times*, 19 October 1997, sec. 14, p. 22.

[27]Rev. Orlo J. Price, "100 Years of Protestantism in Rochester," *Centennial History of Rochester, New York*, vol. 3 (1933), p. 257n; Amy Hanmer-Croughton, "Anti-Slavery Days in Rochester," *Rochester Historical Society Publications*, vol. 14 (1936), p. 113.

[28]Williams-Myers, "The African Presence in the Mid-Hudson Valley," p. 34.

notes, continued

[29]A. Judd Northrup, "Slavery in New York," *State Library Bulletin*, History No. 4 (May 1900), p. 283; Olson, "Negro Slavery in New York," pp. 98-99.

[30]Llewelyn Powys, *Henry Hudson* (New York: Harper, 1928), p. 109; Thomas E. Burke, Jr., *Mohawk Frontier: The Dutch Community of Schenectady, New York, 1661-1710* (Ithaca, NY: Cornell Univ. Press, 1991), pp. 125-26; Kammen, *Colonial New York*, p. 285.

[31]Olson, "Negro Slavery in New York," pp. 162, 163; William Jay, *The Life of John Jay*, vol. 1 (New York, 1833), p. 235; Davis, "Slavery in Colonial New York City," p. 210; Shane White, *Somewhat More Independent: The End of Slavery in New York City, 1770-1810* (Athens, Georgia: Univ. of Georgia Press, 1991), pp. 9-10; Nathaniel Weyl and William Marina, *American Statesmen on Slavery and the Negro* (New Rochelle: Arlington House, 1971), pp. 57-63; Rob N. Weston, "Alexander Hamilton and the Abolition of Slavery in New York, *Afro-Americans in New York Life and History*," vol. 18, no. 1 (January 1994), pp. 34-35.

[32]Dixon Ryan Fox, "The Negro Vote in Old New York," *Political Science Quarterly*, vol. 32 (1917), p. 255.

[33]Olson, "Negro Slavery in New York," p. 190; Linda K. Kerber, "Abolitionists and Amalgamators: The New York City Race Riots of 1834," *New York History*, vol. 48, no. 1 (January 1967), p. 29; Leo H. Hirsch, Jr., "The Negro and New York, 1783-1865," *Journal of Negro History*, vol. 16, no. 4, (October 1931), p. 465.

[34]Hirsch, "The Negro and New York," pp. 390-91, 395-96.

"Free" Blacks in Early New York

The expression "free Blacks" is indicative of the profound elasticity of the term "freedom." The truth is that early Black New Yorkers, as in every northern state, never experienced even a modicum of what could reasonably be considered "freedom." The actual conditions suffered by "free Blacks," whose population never amounted to more than 100 in the colonial period, often made slavery a truly desirable alternative. In fact, the history of the Black "freeman" is barely discernible from that of his brothers and sisters in chattel slavery. After the American Revolution of 1776 this wretched reality only intensified.[1]

Certainly, the law made easy the swift return of Blacks to the status of slave. With skewed memories of the "Negro Plots" of 1712 and 1741 fresh in mind, a large, unsupervised class of Blacks became less and less tolerable to New York whites. "Freedom" under the Dutch and English was bad enough, but the American form of Black "freedom" was bitterly described half a century after the Revolution:

> What an empty name: What a mockery! Free man indeed! When so unrighteously deprived of every civil and political privilege. Free indeed, when almost every honourable incentive to the pursuit of happiness, so largely and so freely held out to his *Fairer* brother, is withheld from him. A freeman, when prejudice binds the most galling chains around him!...What a sad perversion of the term freeman!...Persecuted, and degraded, he wanders along through this land of *universal liberty and equality*, a desolated being. His, no station of honour, power, or fame! Too often the virtuous and intelligent man of colour must drag out

an ignoble life, the victim of poverty, and sorrow. Then unwept for but by a few of his persecuted race, drops into the grave....[2]

A great advocate of poor New York Blacks saw then what historians prefer to ignore today—that "the cruel, killing, Heaven-defying prejudice of which [Blacks] are victims, has closed against them the avenues to riches and respectability—to happiness and usefulness."[3]

Blacks often confronted violent racial hostility. In 1830 whites set their dogs on Black students of the African Free School. They seized a Black girl and almost tore all her clothes off. Black business owners were sometimes assaulted by white mobs. They disrupted Black religious meetings and social functions at will.[4] On the eve of the Civil War, ostensibly fought to "free" Black people, the condition of the Union's "free" Blacks had still not changed.

They suffered indignities unknown to the truly free man. "Everywhere the Negro, whatever his wealth or education or talents, is excluded from social equality and social freedom," wrote one observer. "There were many instances of individual enterprise, however, but these often meant little since Negroes had such a little knowledge of business that white persons often defrauded them out of what they accumulated."[5]

Even so great and noble a leader as Sojourner Truth fell victim to the racial open-season. She had accumulated money which she intended to be used by "all needy and faithful free Negroes." She was persuaded to withdraw her money to invest in a fund for this purpose. The white persuader, a Mr. Pierson, absconded with the money, leaving no recourse for Ms. Truth.[6]

"Free" Blacks: Substandard Housing

Throughout the European domination of the area the settlers manifested a lingering hatred for New York Blacks. The colonial Assembly made this clear from the start when it declared that "no Negro, Indian or Mullatto that shall hereafter be made free shall...possess any Houses, Lands, Tenements, or

Hereditaments." Indeed, the lands awarded to the earliest Black slaves after their sham "manumission," ultimately wound up as part of large farms owned by white aristocrats, and the Trinity Church.[7]

There was little interest in examining, much less improving, the living conditions of New York Blacks. They were confined to the cellars and attics of their employers and to the worst of the city's dwellings. A medical report about the area near Bancker Street illustrates the result of New York's housing policy. "Out of the 48 blacks, living in ten cellars, 33 were sick, of whom 14 died; while, out of 120 whites, living immediately over their heads in the apartments of the same houses, not one even had the fever." Epidemics ravaged New York in the early nineteenth century, made worse by the accumulating water in the cellars and the garbage that littered the pre-garbage-collection city. Blacks suffered inordinately from these infectious diseases.[8]

Still, Blacks showed remarkable resiliency in the hardest of times. Frederick Law Olmsted wrote that during the extreme winter of 1854-55, he did not see a single Black among the thousands of applicants for charity.

> The Negro seems to be more provident than the Celt. The poor blacks always manage to keep themselves more decent and comfortable than poor whites. They very rarely complain, or ask for charity...

Olmsted even reports cases where Blacks shared their food with impoverished whites.[9]

"Free" Blacks: Forced Criminality

Blackwell's Island held New York City's lower class criminals—City Hall held the upper-class ones. "Freedom" offered no acceptable role for Black people, the Constitution having not yet reached their daily reality. "Lawlessness" among Blacks increased under these conditions, though never approaching that of the corrupt white leaders. Nearly 16% of the inmates on the Island were Blacks even though they constituted only 5% of the city's population. A quarter of men committed for vagrancy were Black. The statewide percentages were similar. "Free" Blacks were often imprisoned without formal charges and white vigilante mobs roamed the city for dispossessed Black "freemen" to attack, one such group calling itself "The Rotten Egg Society."[10]

"Free" Blacks: Restricted Employment Options

The difference between slavery and "freedom" is, of course, equal employment opportunity and fair wages for labor performed. If that is the standard, nineteenth century New York Blacks never actually emerged from slavery. Firmly established on the bottom rung of the social and economic ladder, they were barred from the professions and eventually were driven from most of the trades. Though few were able to establish a foothold in the trades, as carpenters, cabinetmakers, tobacconists, upholsterers, sailmakers, mariners, house servants, barbers, porters, brickmakers, coachmen, painters, butchers, and bakers, most of the "inferior" labor was done by Blacks. In the early 1800s Blacks alone collected and disposed of the excrement from white people's outhouses, and they were the city's only chimney sweeps. They most often found employment by slave owners, who hired them to work alongside their brothers and sisters who remained chattel slaves. Blacks were not even allowed to trade with their own family members who remained in slavery "on pain of forfeiting treble the value of the article traded for." There was almost no opportunity for the Black man and woman to engage in any economic pursuit. Their educational opportunities were severely limited and their political options were nil.[11]

The 19th-century Jewish immigrants are most often thought of as street vendors pushing carts of wares over the New York cobblestones. But before them, "free" Blacks and slaves were "heavily involved" in selling fruits and vegetables in the city streets and markets, "many coming from Long Island and New Jersey to sell their produce," until legislation forced them out of this enterprise.[12]

"Free" Blacks: Laws & Mistreatment

> *It seemed unthinkable to whites that Negroes might be accorded courtesies by dignitaries or that they had any right to request them.*[13]

The myth of the "free" Black serves the larger false concept that slavery civilized the Black race, and once the Blacks *earned* their freedom, they were welcomed among the cultured white society. Several incidents in New York history indicate an alternative interpretation:

- When a "gentlemanly" Black sought to shake Daniel Webster's hand in a crowd of whites, their reaction was so severe "he shrunk back in an instant as if electrified."

- The great orator and freedom fighter Frederick Douglass was physically assaulted when he walked down Broadway on "terms of equality" with two white people.

- Douglass recounted a New York boat trip where Blacks had to stay on deck at all hours and in all weather. On Hudson River steamers, he says, Blacks are "compelled sometimes to stroll the deck nearly all night, before they can get a place to lie down, and that place frequently unfit for a dog's accommodation."[14]

- In Harriet Jacobs' book *Incidents in the Life of a Slave Girl*, published in 1861, she wrote of being a nursemaid accompanying a New York City family. On a Hudson River steamboat Jacobs went into the dining hall with the other nursemaids and children when a waiter shouted at her, "Get up! You know you are not allowed to sit here." She refused to leave but she was not served. Later, at a restaurant in Troy the landlord of an inn at which they stopped for breakfast refused to serve her in the dining room.

Jim Crow segregation was the order of the day, in New York. There were Black pews in the churches, Black seats in the courtrooms, Black balconies in the theaters. Blacks were restricted from the ballot box and their presence was unwelcome in public schools, and in the seats of public transportation. "Free" Blacks could not even entertain their still enslaved family members without risking steep fines. The white man's fine for commingling with slaves was half that for "free" Blacks.[15] Historian Linda K. Kerber summarized the New York version of "freedom":

> The American belief that "God himself separated the white from the black" was to be found everywhere, "in the hospitals where humans suffer, in the churches where they pray, in the prisons where they repent, in the cemeteries where they sleep the eternal sleep."[16]

Small white boys solemnly told one another that "if you kicked a Negro's shins, his nose would bleed."[17]

"Free" Blacks: New York Uncle Tomism

There can be no greater role model for the Uncle Tom of today than New York's own Jupiter Hammon (1720-1800). Many a boot-licking political prostitute has had his tongue guided firmly around the soles of white footwear by this happy slave from Queen's Village, Long Island. Whites clearly treasured their prize and made him one of the earliest published negro writers. Born a slave, Hammon passed his entire life as the property of the wealthy and influential Lloyd family. In his "Address to the Negroes of the State of New York," Hammon admonishes the Blacks who improperly think of freedom:

> It may seem hard for us if we think our masters wrong in holding us slaves to obey in all things, but who of us dare dispute with God! He has commanded us to obey, and we ought to do it cheerfully and freely....for my own part I do not wish to

be free; for many of us who are grown up slaves have always had masters to take care of themselves; and it may be for our own comfort to remain as we are.

Here is a sample of his most oft-published poetry:

A Dialogue Entitled the Kind Master and the Dutiful Servant
Master: Come my servant, follow me,
According to thy place;
and surely God will be with thee
And send the heav'nly grace
Servant: Dear Master, I will follow thee
According to thy word.[18]

"Free" Blacks: Spirit of Independence

In the late 1700s, free-spirited Blacks headed for the mountains to try to establish some measure of self-rule. Freemenville was settled by these freed Blacks, who also called their town Guinea, very likely after that region in West Africa from which many may have been kidnapped.[19]

In the next century, activist Gerrit Smith developed a plan to address the economic poverty among Black New Yorkers. His plan for the distribution of 3,000 parcels of land of 40 or 60 acres each pre-dated the government 40-acres-and-a-mule scam of decades later. The land was located in the counties of Franklin, Essex, Hamilton, Fulton, Oneida, Delaware, Madison, and Ulster. A combination of problems such as bad soil, a forbidding climate and unprepared settlers converged to doom the project.[20]

"Free" Blacks: Acts of Rebellion

Despite the web of oppressive laws and customs New York Blacks never accepted their prescribed role. They engaged in a series of passive and aggressive rebellions designed to maintain their dignity and to protest and even undermine the corrupt racial authority.

On several occasions New York Blacks rioted against attempts to put Blacks back into chattel slavery. In 1801, about 250 Blacks rioted when a white woman slave owner tried to send her 20 enslaved Blacks illegally out of state to be sold in Virginia. Blacks rose up "to burn the house, murder all the white people in it and take away a number of black slaves." Unfortunately, about 50 white militiamen interceded and only minor property damage occurred before 23 Blacks were arrested for riot. They were "tried" and sentenced to 60 days in the prison dungeon. Ultimately, the case against the woman was dropped and she once again took custody of her slaves.[21]

In 1826 Southern slavecatchers sued to return an entire family into slavery. After they won in court, they were confronted by Blacks assembled outside, who bombarded them with bricks, sticks, and stones. One officer intercepted a brick with his head, breaking the bridge of his nose, and "disfigur[ing] him in a frightful manner."[22]

"Free" Blacks: Culture and Style

New York Blacks were able to develop a certain style that was indicative of a spirit of independence in the midst of physical repression. Blacks used their unique style to construct their own subculture.[23]

It often started with their names. Generally, the dehumanized Africans carried no surnames until they were "freed," at which time they usually took the name of their captor. Blacks were given comical names by white masters designed in mockery of the Black race. Names like Caesar, Romeo, Flummary, Othello or Pleasant Queen Anne appear often in the colonial record. In response to this indignity, Blacks developed their own system of nomenclature, which is discussed by Shane White in his study of runaway slave advertisements. "One runaway, for example, was a 'man named Cato but calls himself Curtis Johnson'; another 'named York, calls himself Jacob'..." Though given just one name by the white man, some Blacks gave themselves a last name. "Theo. Fowler knew his slave as Scip, but '[a]mongst the black people he goes by the name Scipeo Bailey.'" As White notes, surnames were a sign of freedom. Overwhelmingly, Blacks chose very common and neutral surnames like Johnson, Williams, Smith and Thomas. The use of such surnames likely reflected a desire for anonymity, which, says White, helped draw rural Blacks to the metropolis.[24]

The uniqueness of the Black male walk was described by whites more than two centuries ago. Sam had "a very wide remarkable walk." Will, a New Jersey runaway, "throws out his feet and toes in a singular manner walking very wide." Tom walked "loggy leaning forward." Nat had a "remarkable waddle in his walk, which makes him appear as if he was wounded in the hips." White's study found that other phrases such as "a kind of rocking in his walk," or a "peculiar swing in his gait," or "an awkward swaggering walk," or "walks with a strut" were used to describe the unmistakable glide of the Black man in early New York.[25]

Even the popular breakdance craze of the 1980s is much older than previously believed. Enslaved Blacks used to engage in what they called breakdown contests, which were performed on a plank in front of cheering crowds.[26]

"Free" Blacks: Mis-Education

Most New Yorkers heartily agreed with newspaperman James Gordon Bennett's thoughts of Blacks, "on whom education, and every other means of moral enlightenment have been tried in vain."[27] Despite this dim assessment it was reluctantly agreed that some thought-control would be necessary for better management of the sizable "free" Black population. The job was left to New York's moral reformers, whose goal was law and order, not intellectual elevation.

According to historian Raymond A. Mohl, the school system was aimed at the inculcation of accepted behavior and values and the creation of a sober and contented, hard-working and law-abiding lower class....By demanding ethical conformity, by providing models of decency and decorum, by imposing values upon the lower classes from above, they become protectors of the social order.[28]

In early Black "education," teacher turnover was high; the lessons "too often consisted of parroted Scripture passages." And as for the expectations for young Black matriculators: "In most cases backbreaking labor was their outlook, their only outlook."[29]

Nevertheless, an 1842 report found that the average grade of the white boys in the eighth and ninth classes was 2.32 and of the Blacks in the same classes 2.47.[30]

In 1858 the State of New York spent nearly $4 million on schools, and of this only $10,729.93 went to the Black schools. The following year, in a fit of unbridled magnanimity, this amount was more than doubled. Blacks, who represented 1.3% of the population, received 0.47% of the education budget.

New York City was no different. It spent $1.6 million on public schools for whites, and a mere $1,000 on Black public schools. Showing an uncanny similarity to the condition of today's schools, the white schools were described as "commodious and elegant," while those of Blacks were in "filthy and degraded neighborhoods, dark, damp, small, and cheerless, safe neither for the morals nor for the health of those who are compelled to go to them, if they go anywhere, and calculated rather to repel than to attract them."[31]

African Free Schools: The New York African Free School was founded in 1786, established by the New York Manumission Society to divert Black children from "the slippery paths of vice" and to make them "quiet and orderly citizens."[32] Even the Society's abolitionist leader, John Jay, had low expectations of his pitiable Black clients. To an associate he wrote:

As to the eventual fate of the children, it is important that they be not left entirely either to their parents or to themselves, it being difficult to give them morals, manners, and habits. These can only be learned from reality.[33]

The school had no intention of making Black children into doctors, engineers or scientists; instead the school's intent was to make them "more orderly and tractable as they emerged from slavery." After a suitable amount of training, "graduates" were bound out as sailors, apprentices, and domestic servants.[34]

Nonetheless, the African Free School became central to the Black New Yorker's training process. Black students demonstrated a thirst for knowledge and a discipline that was reflected in this observation in the *Commercial Advertiser*: "We never beheld a white school of the same age, (of and under fifteen), in which, without exception, there was more order and neatness of dress, and cleanliness of person." The article further pointed out that of the 700 pupils, 264 were capable of reading.[35]

Soon, Black New Yorkers directly challenged the aims of the school as inadequate. In the late 1820s, in a foreshadowing of the school battles of the 1960s, Black community leaders demanded a say in determining the educational policies at the African Free Schools and initiated a boycott.

The white man that ran the schools, Charles Andrews, was pressured to resign in 1832 when it was learned that he had developed the opinion that Blacks ought to go back to Africa. White school administrators explained that his departure was the result of "prejudice now existing against him in the black community."[36]

Blacks insisted that Black men and women teach their children. James Adams, a Black man, replaced Andrews and attendance at the African Free Schools climbed above 500 for the first time.

The Manumission Society countered such boldness by transferring its schools to the Public School Society, which made sweeping changes without consulting the Black community leaders, parents or students. Most of the Black teachers were discharged by the new trustees, among other changes resented by Blacks. They vigorously protested and their Black teachers were reappointed, and enrollments began to improve.[37]

By 1834 seven African schools had been established throughout the city. Other efforts produced at least 74 Black schools throughout the state.[38]

In Rochester, there were no legal barriers against the enrollment of Blacks in the school system. In 1834, however, the school committee found that "the colored scholar can hardly prosper." It stated plainly that "his mind is in chains, and he is a slave." Local parents successfully petitioned to form an African School.[39]

Buffalo Blacks sent their children to sit-in at local schools, but the school officials physically forced them out. State Superintendent John Spencer concurred with the schools' approach to keeping Black children out of the local schools. "The admissions of colored children," he said, "is in many places so odious that whites will not attend." Alderman O. G. Steele demanded that Blacks be ejected from public schools:

> They [the blacks] must be looked upon with aversion and treated with more or less opprobrium and their progress in their studies must be retarded rather than advanced in the public schools.[40]

In 1848, Buffalo School Superintendent Samuel Caldwell physically ejected Black children from the public schools. Drawing on his Hamitic training, he reasoned that "[t]hey require...longer training and severer discipline...and generations must elapse before they will possess the vigor of intellect, the power of memory and judgment, that are so early developed in the Anglo-Saxon race." Strong Black leaders were frustrated by the imposition of "moderate" uncle toms as spokespersons for the Buffalo community—a tactic still in widespread and successful use today. White officials used the hand-crafted division to "cite the difference of opinion among the colored people" as the reason for refusing to change their policies.[41]

Superintendent of Schools John S. Fosdick provides a good example of the kind of white friends Blacks were "blessed" with in New York. A "conductor" on the Underground Railroad, Fosdick described integrationist Blacks as "mischievous agitators," and diligently sought to enforce Section 5 of Buffalo's 1853 Charter, which stated that "all public schools organized in the city of Buffalo shall be free to all white children." Blacks, seeking education for their children, defied the ban on their school attendance and the outraged Fosdick moved into action by physically expelling Blacks from the schools.[42]

One Black girl alleged in a court action that Fosdick, "with force and violence...did drag her out of her seat and violently shoved, pushed, beat, and struck her, driving her away from the school." Ultimately, the State Supreme Court in 1868 found in favor of defendant Fosdick "with costs adjusted at $192.48." Buffalo Blacks never succeeded in obtaining integration. A separate white-run school for Blacks, they called an "African school," was established in a ward where only 10 percent of Buffalo's Blacks resided. Frederick Douglass described such a school as "a low, damp, dark cellar better fit for an ice house." Buffalo's superintendent, however, described the building as "the good effect of the enlightened and liberal policy of the Common Council." In 1880, the Buffalo Common Council closed western New York's last "African school."[43]

"Free" Blacks: Political Wrongs

Blacks struggled long and hard for political rights in the pigsty that passed for the New York political arena. Even before the end of legal slavery in New York, Blacks began to agitate for their voting rights in the political world.

The Eurocentric history of New York records that Blacks were granted the right to vote in 1811. Our Afrocentric history shows that this "right" was accompanied by some additional responsibilities whites did not have:

1) Blacks were required to obtain a "certificate of freedom" from a New York judge;

2) A paid lawyer was required for this purpose;

3) Twenty-five cents was to be paid by the Black applicant to the court;

4) The judge giving the certificate was to be paid a shilling;

5) Another shilling was to be paid to the County Clerk for filing the certificate in his office;

6) An additional payment was to be made to the Clerk, for the certificate to be used by the voter.

Such devious political maneuvers and an equally cynical historical whitewash lead many to assume that the low Black voter turnout was due to apathy rather than the real economic barriers installed by white power barons.[44]

By 1819 there were nearly 11,000 Blacks in the city of New York but only 100 were allowed to vote in the election of that year. The rich white folks' party, or Federalists, formed an alliance with their former slaves in what appeared as an earnest effort to ensure "the political rights of all Americans." Federalists realized that Blacks, voting as a bloc, could sway a New York election, and they sought to control the Black ballot.[45]

All whites were not happy with this new alliance.

• Genessee County delegate John Z. Ross said that the Blacks were "incapable of...exercising that privilege with any sort of discretion....They have no just conception of civil liberty." He claimed that granting Blacks the right to vote would mean a stampeding of Blacks to New York. He accurately declared that whites who favored Black suffrage did so because they wanted to control the Black vote.

- Col. Samuel Young, of Saratoga County, bitterly opposed Black voting rights and wanted it stated in the Constitution.

- Chief Justice Ambrose Spencer, representing Albany County, declared that Blacks "lacked intelligence," just like children, and should be excluded from the polls.

- Mr. P. A. Livingston, of Dutchess County, said that 20 of the fifty Blacks who had presented a petition asking for equal voting rights, "could not even write their names—and those petitioners were doubtless of the most respectable of the color."

- He and Jacob Radcliff, of New York City, further asserted that the "criminality" of Blacks disqualified them from consideration.

- J. L. Russell of St. Lawrence County said that 90% of his constituents, including the abolitionists, believe that "the Almighty had created the black man inferior to the white man...They believe our own white race was the only one capable of self-government."

- John H. Hunt of New York City said that the Bible forbade the yoking together of different animals, and claimed that it was just as bad "to unite the Caucasian and the Negro races in the same government."

- Mr. Horatio J. Stow of Erie County asked his colleagues in the Convention if they "would pull down the working class of men by bringing them in contact with a degraded race."[46]

By a narrow margin in 1821, the delegates at the Constitutional Convention in Albany decided to require Black voters to be landowners of $250 worth of property and residents of at least three years—a requirement not applied to whites.[47]

In 1838 the New York Association for the Political Elevation and Improvement of People of Color was established to be one of the first organizations that was, by design, uncorrupted by white money. This attitude represented a new phase in Black self-determination—a budding predecessor of the Marcus Garvey movement of the next century.[48]

Notes

[1] Shane White, "'We Dwell in Safety and Pursue Our Honest Callings': Free Blacks in New York City, 1783-1810," *Journal of American History*, vol. 75, no. 2 (September 1988), pp. 448, 452; Thomas Joseph Davis, "Slavery in Colonial New York City" (Ph.D. diss., Columbia Univ., 1974), p. 112; Rhoda Golden Freeman, *The Free Negro in New York City in the Era Before the Civil War* (New York: Garland, 1994), p. 5; Ralph R. Ireland, "Slavery on Long Island: A Study of Economic Motivation," *Journal of Long Island History*, vol. 6, no. 1, pp. 9-10; Herman D. Bloch, "The New York Negro's Battle For Political Rights, 1777-1865," *International Review of Social History*, vol. 9 (1964), p. 65.

[2] Freeman, *The Free Negro in New York City*, pp. 9, 67-68.

[3] Zita Dyson, "Gerrit Smith's Efforts in Behalf of the Negroes in New York," *Journal of Negro History*, vol. 3, no. 4 (October 1918), p. 357.

[4] Paul Gilje, *The Road to Mobocracy* (Univ. of North Carolina Press, 1987), pp. 157-58.

[5] Arnett G. Lindsay, "The Economic Condition of the Negroes of New York Prior to 1861," *Journal of Negro History*, vol. 6, no. 2 (April 1921), p. 196; Charles H. Wesley, "The Negroes of New York in the Emancipation Movement," *Journal of Negro History*, vol. 24, no. 1 (January 1939), p. 66.

[6] Arnett G. Lindsay, "The Economic Condition of the Negroes," pp. 196-197.

[7] Davis, "Slavery in Colonial New York City," p. 113; Freeman, *The Free Negro in New York City* p. 8; Edith Evans Asbury, "Freed Black Farmers Tilled Manhattan's Soil in the 1600's," *The New York Times*, 7 December 1977, sec. B.

[8] White, "'We Dwell in Safety,'" p. 466.

[9] Leo H. Hirsch, Jr., "The Negro and New York, 1783-1865," *Journal of Negro History*, vol. 16, no. 4 (October 1931), p. 435.

[10] Hirsch, "The Negro and New York," p. 440; Douglas Greenberg, "Patterns of Criminal Prosecution in Eighteenth-Century New York," *New York History*, vol. 56, no. 2 (April 1975), pp. 146-147; Ireland, "Slavery on Long Island," pp. 9-10.

[11] Rennie Simson, "A Community in Turmoil: Black American Writers in New York State Before the Civil War," *Afro-Americans in New York Life and History*, vol. 13, no. 1 (January 1989), p. 57; Hirsch, "The Negro and New York," pp. 436, 438; Federal Writers' Project, *New York Panorama* (New York: Random House, 1938; reprint, 1984), p. 134; Lindsay, "The Economic Condition of the Negroes," pp. 195, 198; White, "'We

notes, continued

Dwell in Safety'," pp. 453-55; Paul A. Gilje, "Between Slavery and Freedom: New York African Americans in the Early Republic," review of *Somewhat More Independent: The End of Slavery in New York City, 1770-1810*, by Shane White, *Reviews in American History* 20 (June 1992), p. 166. It is likely that the few Blacks in the professions were from the favored class of light-skinned Blacks, called "mulattos," whose appearance was less frightening to elite whites who held power over educational opportunities for aspiring clerks, doctors, lawyers, merchants and teachers. See Shane White, *Somewhat More Independent: The End of Slavery in New York City, 1770-1810* (Athens, Georgia: Univ. of Georgia Press, 1991), pp. 12, 47; Carl Nordstrom, "The New York Slave Code," *Afro-Americans in New York Life and History*, vol. 4, no. 1 (January 1980), p. 15; Edwin Vernon Morgan, "Slavery in New York, with Special Reference to New York City," *Slavery in the States: Selected Essays* (New York: Negro Universities Press, 1969), p. 11; *The Colonial Laws of New York from the Year 1664 to the Revolution*, vol. 2 (Albany, 1894), p. 679; Nordstrom, "The New York Slave Code," pp. 10, 15; Freeman, *The Free Negro in New York City*, p. 76.

[12]White, "'We Dwell in Safety'," p. 456; Edwin Olson, "Negro Slavery in New York, 1626-1827" (Ph.D. thesis, New York Univ., 1938), pp. 88, 135-36; Kenneth Jackson, ed., *Encyclopedia of New York City* (Yale Univ. Press, 1995), p. 1076.

[13]Freeman, *The Free Negro in New York City*, p. 70.

[14]Freeman, *The Free Negro in New York City*, pp. 70, 75; Hirsch, "The Negro and New York," pp. 424-25.

[15]Linda K. Kerber, "Abolitionists and Amalgamators: The New York City Race Riots of 1834," *New York History*, vol. 48, no. 1 (January 1967), pp. 28-29; Carl Nordstrom, "The New York Slave Code," p. 15.

[16]Kerber, "Abolitionists and Amalgamators," pp. 28-29.

[17]Edward Robb Ellis, *The Epic of New York City* (New York: Coward-McCann, 1966), p. 235.

[18]Simson, "A Community in Turmoil," p. 58; Roi Ottley and William J. Weatherby, eds., *The Negro in New York: An Informal Social History* (Dobbs Ferry, NY: Oceana Publications, 1967), p. 34; Hirsch, "The Negro and New York," pp. 384-85.

[19]A.J. Williams-Myers, "The African Presence in the Mid-Hudson Valley Before 1800: A Preliminary Historiographical Sketch," *Afro-Americans in New York Life and History*, vol. 8, no. 1 (January 1984), p. 34.

[20]Lindsay, "The Economic Condition of the Negroes," pp. 194-95.

[21]Gilje, *The Road to Mobocracy*, pp. 146, 147, 149, 150.

[22]Gilje, *The Road to Mobocracy*, pp. 151-52.

[23]Shane White, "A Question of Style: Blacks in and around New York City in the Late 18th Century," *Journal of American Folklore*, vol. 102, no. 403 (January-March 1989), p. 24.

[24]Anne Hartell, "Slavery on Long Island," *Nassau County Historical Journal*, vol. 6, no. 2 (fall 1943), p. 59; White, "A Question of Style," pp. 28, 29.

[25]White, "A Question of Style," p. 35.

[26]White, "A Question of Style," p. 33; Edwin Olson, "Negro Slavery in New York," pp. 141-42.

[27]Dixon Ryan Fox, "The Negro Vote in Old New York," *Political Science Quarterly*, vol. 32 (1917), p. 267n.

notes, continued

[28]Raymond A. Mohl, "Education as Social Control in New York City, 1784-1825," *New York History*, vol. 51, no. 3 (April 1970), pp. 236-37.

[29]Eve Thurston, "Ethiopia Unshackled: A Brief History of the Education of Negro Children in New York City," *Bulletin of the New York Public Library*, vol. 69, no. 4 (April 1965), p. 218.

[30]Hirsch, "The Negro and New York," p. 431.

[31]Hirsch, "The Negro and New York," pp. 427-28.

[32]Gilje, *The Road to Mobocracy*, p. 156; John L. Rury, "The New York African Free School, 1827-1836: Conflict Over Community Control of Black Education," *Phylon*, vol. 44, no. 3 (1983), p. 187; Mohl, "Education as Social Control," pp. 225-26.

[33]Thurston, "Ethiopia Unshackled," p. 216.

[34]Rury, "The New York African Free School," p. 187; Mohl, "Education as Social Control in New York City," p. 224; Lindsay, "The Economic Condition of the Negroes," p. 192.

[35]Hirsch, "The Negro and New York," p. 429; Lindsay, "The Economic Condition of the Negroes of New York," p. 193n. See also James Weldon Johnson, *Black Manhattan* (New York: Atheneum, 1930; reprint, 1968), p. 23.

[36]Rury, "The New York African Free School," pp. 187, 191-92.

[37]Rury, "The New York African Free School," pp. 193, 194-96.

[38]Mohl, "Education as Social Control," p. 225; Carleton Mabee, "A List of the First Black Schools in Each Place in New York State, From Colonial Times to 1945," *Afro-Americans in New York Life and History*, vol. 2, no. 2 (July 1978), p. 14; Hirsch, "The Negro and New York," p. 432.

[39]Arthur O. White, "The Black Movement Against Jim Crow Education in Buffalo, New York, 1800-1900," *Phylon*, vol. 30, no. 4 (1969), p. 376.

[40]White, "The Black Movement Against Jim Crow Education," pp. 380, 381.

[41]White, "The Black Movement Against Jim Crow Education," p. 382.

[42]White, "The Black Movement Against Jim Crow Education," pp. 387, 391n.

[43]White, "The Black Movement Against Jim Crow Education," pp. 376-78, 389, 390, 391, 393.

[44]Charles H. Wesley, "Negro Suffrage in the Period of Constitution-Making: 1787-1865," *Journal of Negro History*, vol. 32, no. 2 (April 1947), p. 157.

[45]Hirsch, "The Negro and New York," pp. 417-18; Wesley, "Negro Suffrage," p. 155.

[46]Hirsch, "The Negro and New York," pp. 418-19, 422.

[47]Hirsch, "The Negro and New York," p. 420; Wesley, "Negro Suffrage," pp. 159-60.

[48]Daniel Perlman, "Organizations of the Free Negro in New York City, 1800-1860," *Journal of Negro History*, vol. 56, no. 3 (July 1971), pp. 189-90.

New York Blacks in the Civil War Era

There is a commonly held belief among Americans that the Civil War was fought to "end slavery" and that Northerners laid down their lives for Black people. The history of New York is proof of the absurdity of that bizarre notion. As the war between the North and South approached in the 1850s, New York City's 12,000 Blacks found that they were targets of hatred of both sides. Most white New Yorkers, wrote historian Adrian Cook, "continued to nourish an intense hatred of Negroes."[1] According to *A Short History of New York*,

> [n]either the outbreak of war nor the Emancipation Proclamation brought better times for the Negroes of New York....Prejudice against the Negroes was common among most citizens of New York.[2]

To truly understand why the misconception has survived so long, it is important to examine New York's close relationship with its alleged "enemy."

Civil War: New Yorkers and Southern Slavery

> *When the London Times asked De Bow what he thought New York would be like without slavery, he replied, "The ships would rot at her docks; grass would grow in Wall Street and Broadway, and the glory of New York, like that of Babylon and Rome, would be numbered with the things of the past.[3]*

New York loved slavery! The most opulent plantation houses of the Cotton Kingdom were not in Virginia, Tennessee or the Carolinas; they were in downtown Manhattan. In fact, New York dominated every single phase of the cotton trade from plantation to market.[4] Consider these facts:

- As soon as Blacks emerged from the fields with sacks bulging with cotton, New York traders were there to pay the white plantation masters by the bale.

- Ships hired and insured by New York firms and sailed by New York crews most often carried the cotton to New York and New England for worldwide distribution.

- As much as 40¢ of every dollar in the sale of cotton went to New Yorkers who never had to see a plantation, plant a seed or beat a slave.

- The cash advances necessary for the planting of the new crop came from New York firms and banks.

- In New York City, a vast number of legal, financial, and clerical workers handled the voluminous paper work involved in the slave trade.

- The merchandise consumed in the plantation South came mainly from New York. Historian Leo Hershkowitz wrote that "New York City's relationship to the South was an intimate one," and that "[t]he metropolis was probably as much like a southern community as could be found along the northeastern seaboard."

- Industries that supported the plantation economy, like mining and railroads, were owned and financed by New York businessmen.

- Foreclosed plantations made New York bankers owners of thousands of Black slaves. One partner in "a Broadway firm" was said to possess twelve hundred slaves, and another had three hundred.

A Southern economist claimed in 1860 that, "All the profitable branches of freighting, brokering, selling, banking, insurance, etc., that grow out of the Southern product are enjoyed in New York." New York was "almost as dependent upon Southern slavery as Charleston itself," said another.

Plantation slavery was big business—New York was like the corporate headquarters and the entire plantation South was like the factory floor. The Southern economy was controlled entirely by New York businessmen. It has been estimated that in 1861 Southern slave-holding interests owed New York merchants about $200 million.[5]

Civil War: **The Real Cause of the Rebellion**

The growing antagonism between North and South was, in fact, due to this trade imbalance, which Southerners thought grossly unfair. The Southerners felt that they were at the mercy of Northern businessmen (and they were) and sought to free themselves even by armed rebellion. The New Orleans *Crescent* bitterly labeled New York, "the center of reckless speculation, unflinching fraud and downright robbery."[6]

Southerners made several unsuccessful attempts to bypass New York merchants by establishing direct trade with foreign cotton buyers like England. They spoke of building Southern ports with banks that would handle Southern financial affairs in the South. This scenario frightened New Yorkers, who knew that the loss of Southern trade meant total ruin. The desperate cry of "Save the Union," meant, in reality, save the precious money flow from the plantation to the New York and other Northern merchants. Frankly, no group had more to lose by a Southern rebellion than the businessmen of New York.[7]

For this reason, New York merchants made every effort to reassure their white Southern brethren of their full support and highest regard, as well as their disdain for the "fanatical," "demagogic" abolitionists. The bowing and scraping of New York merchants and politicians was limitless. Banker August Belmont told Southerners that their fugitive slave property would be promptly returned and that they could count on an equal right to slavery in the newly-settled western territories.[8] To these greedy New York profiteers the meddling abolitionists represented the Devil himself. One of them told

Samuel J. May, a prominent abolitionist, exactly what he thought:

> Mr. May, we are not such fools as not to know that slavery is a great evil, a great wrong....[But, w]e cannot afford, sir, to let you and your associates endeavor to overthrow slavery. It is not a matter of principles with us. It is a matter of business necessity....We mean, sir, to put you abolitionists down, by fair means if we can, by foul means if we must.[9]

In this pro-slavery atmosphere, it is easy to see how New York Blacks were physically scapegoated and their interests abused.

Civil War: New York, Lincoln and Black Rights

> *Electors, remember that a vote for Lincoln is a vote to make a negro equal to a white man.*[10]

The events surrounding the 1860 election provide plenty of evidence that the North and the South were the best of friends when it came to their ideas and policies toward Black folks. The election would decide if Lincoln would be president and if New York Blacks should have voting rights.

Few New Yorkers liked "Honest Abe." His policies seemed likely to initiate the threatened Civil War—which meant serious economic losses to the industrial and commercial interests of New York. Everyone, from the politicians to the press to the clergy to the business leaders, decried a Lincoln victory. The *Herald* called Lincoln a "vulgar, village politician," and warned white people that, "If Lincoln is elected you will have to compete with the labor of four million emancipated negroes."[11]

But Abraham Lincoln was no lover of Black people, though he did *hate them less* than the other candidates. Lincoln himself tried to shake this "soft on niggers" image when he condemned white abolitionist John Brown as a foolish fanatic, but it just wasn't strong enough.[12] He again tried to end the speculation:

I will say that I am not, nor ever have been in favor of bringing about in any way the social and political equality of the white and black races; that I am not nor ever have been in favor of making voters or jurors of negroes, nor to intermarry with white people; and I will say in addition to this that there is a physical difference between the white and black races which I believe will forever forbid the two races living together on terms of social and political equality.[13]

The pro-slavery forces which dominated New York politics were not appeased. Ultimately Lincoln lost badly in New York City, while just barely winning the state.

The White Man's View of Black Voting Rights: The other racially charged issue on the ballot was voting rights for New York Blacks. About 80 percent of Blacks could not vote because of a law which said that Blacks must own property worth $250. For years, Blacks campaigned to remove this qualification from the state constitution, and now the people were going to have a chance to vote on an amendment allowing equal voting rights for Blacks.[14]

Passage was unlikely because even abolitionists did not favor granting political rights to the Black man. (Women of New York would not gain the right to vote until 1917.) The press continued to set the tone for the average white New Yorker:

- *Brooklyn Standard*, on September 22, 1860, said that: "Unadulterated Black Republicanism is bad enough, but political amalgamation with black men is worse." "What occasion is there of our adding to voters in this State 10,000 idle, thieving, ignorant negroes? Let the property qualification stand—let those who are thrifty and industrious vote; but let us have not extension of it to the degraded blacks who infest most of our northern cities."

- The Brooklyn *City News* charged that "there is a natural inferiority on the part of the black race..." It further warned the readers that the proposed legislation unreasonably asked whites "to deposit your vote in the ballot box, cheek by jowl with a large 'buck nigger'."

• The *City News* spoke for the white man: "Remember, conservative men of New York, that you will be called upon...to vote whether ten or fifteen thousand sooty negroes shall be raised to a political level with yourselves in this State."

• The New York *Tribune*, advocated separation in an editorial entitled, "What We Shall Do with the Negro." "The ignorant and servile race," it said, "will not and cannot be emancipated and raised to the enjoyment of equal civil rights with the dominant and intelligent race; they will be driven out."[15]

Civil War: New York Racism

Every segment of New York society spoke up on the issues of the Civil War era. The politicians, the press, business and labor, and even the religious leadership all weighed in with their hateful bigotry.

New York Politicians: Outrageously corrupt, proslavery politicians controlled New York City in the Civil War era. New York City politicians saw little to gain in opposing their southern counterparts. Indeed, the Democrats incited the traditionally anti-Black immigrant to a most vicious racism. They proclaimed an abhorrence equal to any southerner's for the "aggression and insult visited upon [the South] by abolitionists." The city government, known commonly as Tammany Hall, opposed any political favors to Blacks, because it was thought that such privileges would attract more Blacks to New York.[16]

No one was more direct about these issues than the honorable mayor Fernando Wood. He saw nothing wrong with slavery. At the state Democratic convention in February 1860 he said, "The profits, luxuries, the necessities, nay even the physical existence [of New York]...depend upon the products only to be obtained by the continuance of slave labor and the prosperity of the slave master." And later, Mayor Wood and the political leadership opposed the passage of the Thirteenth Amendment ending most forms of slavery in America.[17]

When the nation erupted into civil war, the popular and indomitable mayor called for the secession of the city. The way he saw it, his city paid two-thirds of the expenses of the United States government anyway, and the war was Lincoln's doing. Wood reassured the Confederacy that business would not be interrupted by Lincoln's needless war and that New York still welcomed trade with the South, with open arms.[18] Others were equally committed to the white cause:

- Hiram Ketcham assured Southern whites that if a conflict arose, "the city's residents would stand by their brethren, the white race."

- Charles O'Conor, considered one of the ablest lawyers in the city, argued that "slavery was just and ordained by nature."

- Legendary politician "Boss" Tweed believed that denying the right of white men to own Black slaves was in violation of "Supreme Law."

- New York City congressman John Cochrane proposed legislation designed to preserve slavery in the South.

- Alderman Henry Genet bluntly declared, "Never allow South Carolina or no slave, or no nigger of any description to interfere with our stars." Fighting for a slave, he proclaimed, "was the same as fighting for a horse." "Why, you don't pretend that a nigger is a man, do you?"

- James Gerard, a prominent lawyer and candidate for Congress, warned his "friends from Ireland" that Republicans were abolitionists, and if they were not defeated the result would be "negro labor dragging you from your free labor."[19]

The New York Press: *The New York Evening Day-Book* declared that slavery was "one of the happiest occurrences in human affairs." The Black man, the newspaper said, was in "his natural position of social subordination."

The *Herald* described antislavery efforts as "nigger worship." It promoted the popular view that slaves were like animals and cannibals. The newspaper called Blacks "niggers" and openly claimed that they lacked a "high degree of intellectual development" and were inferior to whites.

The *Evening Post* opined that, "The City of New York belongs almost as much to the South as to the North."

The *Journal of Commerce* claimed that "an inferior race had to be placed in a condition of slavery" and that immediate freedom for the Blacks would create a series of events "too horrible to contemplate."

Alabama politician William Yancey, campaigning in New York for Kentuckian John C. Breckinridge, said that the South asked nothing "but that you will not allow anyone to steal away her niggers," to the delight of a New York crowd. The *Daily News, Herald, Journal of Commerce,* and *Evening Day-Book* eagerly endorsed his candidate.[20]

New York Business and Labor: Just twenty years before the war, most dock workers, coachmen, shoeshiners, barbers, maids, tailors and waiters had been Black people. By 1860 Blacks had been forced out of these jobs and replaced by Irish. Some companies printed circulars warning their employees that a vote for Lincoln cut off their Southern business, and there would be little work and increased Black competition. This, indeed, was a commonly held belief among the white laboring classes. This belief generated the hysteria that led to the mayhem of the New York Draft Riots.[21]

As a rule, New York businessmen endeavored to maintain their profitable relationship with the slave-holding South and to "put down" abolitionists. Not surprisingly, New York City's export merchants dealing chiefly in cotton condemned all anti-slavery movements.[22]

New York resident Samuel Morse, the inventor of the telegraph, believed that slavery was a divine institution, and as a matter of conscience he considered abolition a sin.[23]

New York Religious Leadership: New York religious groups had no qualms about supporting Black slavery. This reality moved one writer to observe that New York's religious behavior "laid bare the misconception so frequently voiced that the God of the North frowned on slavery."

James W. White, an Irish immigrant and New York city judge, founded a Roman Catholic newspaper that stridently defended slavery.[24]

Jews represented about one percent of the city's population but they had 27 synagogues with many congregation members of "considerable influence." The most prominent rabbi in America was Dr. Morris Raphall, who severely criticized the well-known Christian antislavery minister Henry Ward Beecher of Brooklyn: "How dare you denounce slaveholding as a sin. When you remember that Abraham, Isaac, Jacob [and] Job...were slaveholders, does it strike you that you are guilty of something little short of blasphemy?"[25]

The New York Draft Riots

Racial violence has as much a place in the history of New York as in deepest Mississippi.[26] The thirst for Black blood was no less a part of the white New Yorker than the thirst for Jewish blood was for the 20th-century Nazi. The *New-York Evening Post* in 1834 seems to agree:

> The fury of demons seems to have entered the breasts of our misguided populace. Like those ferocious animals which, having once tasted blood, are seized with an insatiable thirst for gore, they have an appetite awakened for outrage, which nothing but the most extensive and indiscriminate destruction seems capable of appeasing. The cabin of the poor Negro, and the temples dedicated to the living God, are alike the objects of their blind

fury. The rights of private and public property, the obligations of law, the authority of its ministers, and even the power of the military, are all equally spurned by these audacious sons of riot and disorder. What will be the next mark of their licentious wrath it is impossible to conjecture.[27]

The threat of Civil War fanned every racist tendency within white New York. When, in 1863, Uncle Sam came looking to fill a Union army recruitment quota of about 30,000 New Yorkers, white males violently objected. The draft exempted rich folks, who simply paid $300 to escape enlistment altogether—which outraged the lower-class whites. They had also been told that the war was being fought "for niggers" and this brought them to a boil.[28]

The contemptuous mostly Irish immigrants were too cowardly to confront Uncle Sam or the white merchant class, for whom the war was really fought. Their natural response was to resort to ruthless violence against helpless Blacks.[29]

Ruthless Violence, White Mayhem: On July 11, 1863, a volatile mix of draft proceedings, bad liquor, and rank hatred initiated the most brutal, most widespread, and most destructive riot in American history.[30]

During the next three days, 70,000 treasonous whites sacked stores, burned the homes of abolitionists and lynched stray Blacks. All were ineffectively repelled (sometimes joined) by 2,000 policemen. Willard A. Heaps provides an overview of the harrowing scene:

> ...the crowds roamed the city without pause in a continuous orgy of destruction. They committed every sort of crime—murder, lynching, looting, and burning. One of the city's newspapers correctly called the riots "a carnival of violence."[31]

Whites packed the street for twelve solid blocks, and within an hour the entire block from Forty-sixth to Forty-seventh streets was in flames. According to the *New York Times*, "the atrocities committed against blacks during the four days of rioting were at least as grotesque as anything that ever emanated from the Deep South." Rioters swarmed into hotels and beat up Black bellboys and waiters. The superintendent of police was "beaten into insensibility," as police were outnumbered 200 to 1.[32] The descriptions of the massacre are horrifying. Below is a sampling of the violence endured by Blacks during the 4-day pogrom.

- William Mealy and Matthew Zweick alternately beat, kicked, and stoned James Costello, a Black man. They trampled his body, and finally hanged him. They then dragged him to a mudhole where one immersed him in water while the other emptied a barrel of ashes over his head.

- George Glass yanked crippled Black coachman Abraham Franklin and his sister Henrietta from their rooms, assaulted the girl and dragged Franklin through the streets and hanged him from a lamppost. The military arrived and cut down Franklin's body, but when the soldiers departed, the corpse was hoisted up again with cheers for Confederate president Jefferson Davis. Patrick Butler then dragged the body through the streets by the genitals as the crowd applauded. After yet another hanging rioters cut off Franklin's fingers and toes.

- The houses of Black residents were often identified by bands of small white boys who "marked" them by stoning the windows. The boys later returned with their male elders to pull out the Black tenants and complete the bloody mission.

- Democratic politician William Cruise gave straw and matches to a gang of white boys and led them around the corner to the rooms of William Derrickson, a Black laborer. Derrickson escaped but his son Alfred was pulled out onto the street, stripped, and beaten. A fire was started under a lamppost, and Alfred would have been lynched and burned to death were it not for the intercession of area residents who chased the rioters away.

- Black workingman Charles Jackson was beaten and nearly drowned.

- Jeremiah Robinson, a Black man trying to escape to Brooklyn, was beaten senseless, his body thrown into the East River.

- Owners of waterfront establishments that catered to Black laborers were stripped of their clothes and threatened with hangings.

- Black sailor William Williams was assaulted when he walked ashore at an Upper West Side pier to ask directions. As he was forced to prostrate, each gang member jumped him, smashed his body with a cobblestone, and finally planted a knife in his chest—to the glee of onlookers.

- Whites invaded a house on East 27th Street and killed W. H. Nichols, a young Black man who was attempting to defend his elderly mother. Unsatisfied, they snatched a newborn Black baby, who had seen all of three days before he was hurled out of the window by the white rioters.

- Several hundred white men and boys seized a helpless Black man, beat him into insensibility, hanged him by a rope thrown over the limb of a tree, hacked his body, and finally built a fire to roast the corpse.

- A Black man was knocked to the ground and held down while a white man repeatedly dropped a twenty-pound rock on his head.

- Three Blacks were lynched on the site of the present Pennsylvania Railroad Station while "a gang of bestial women milled about the dangling bodies of the black men, gashing their flesh with knives, while more than 5,000 men cheered them on."

- On Staten Island fifty white men beat a lame Black man unable to follow his friends into the woods.

- A Black man was hanged from a chestnut tree on Clarkson Street. A gang of white men and boys built a fire under him, "dancing wildly around the roasting flesh."[33]

Those unable to flee bore the brunt of the attack. Black men, women and children were "tortured and slaughtered." Apartments that housed Black families were torched, and the victims' furniture demolished and burned in sidewalk bonfires. According to the *Herald* some 3,000 Blacks gathered about a relief station. "The unfortunate darkies exhibited all the evidence of extreme hunger, and appeared to be suffering greatly from fear." Blacks were chased and cornered and strung up and tortured. "Irish biddies knifed the flesh of hanged Negroes, poured oil into the wounds, set fire to the oil, danced under the human torches, and sang obscene songs." A few whites offered shelter to Blacks who were being pursued by rioters, though most doors were slammed tight.[34]

The Attack on the "Colored Orphan Asylum": With all of the recorded conduct of the demonic white mob, the one atrocity that exceeded even the basest of human savagery was the attack on the Colored Orphan Asylum in New York City.

The home of last resort for about 250 Black children below the age of twelve, the orphanage was a large institutional building on Fifth Avenue between 43rd and 44th streets. When 3,000 marauders set upon the building, there seemed to be little doubt that most of the children would have been butchered if they had not been led out a rear entrance while the mob was breaking down the front door.[35]

Its appetite for blood and melanin not yet quenched, the mob suddenly attacked a group of about twenty children who were cut off from the main group of orphans. One little Black girl, who had been lost in the confusion of the hasty escape, was discovered trembling under a bed. She was pulled out and beaten to death. Ten-year-old orphan Jane Barry was killed when a bureau, dropped from the window of an upper floor, landed on her head.[36] Rabid whites smashed furniture, uprooted trees, shrubbery, and fences before they burned the orphanage to the ground. One observer noted that, "The crowds' desire [was] not merely to destroy but to wipe clean the tangible evidence of a black presence." There was no saving the building—the crowd had cut the hoses of the arriving fire companies.[37]

Counting the Black Bodies: When the smoke cleared and rum kegs emptied, as many as 2,000 people were dead and 8,000 wounded. More than 100 buildings were burned down, and about 200 others were damaged and looted. The property loss "has been estimated variously at from $1.5 to $5 million."[38] Edward Robb Ellis provides this remarkable passage in *The Epic of New York*:

> No one will ever know exactly how many people were killed. The New York *Post* said that the bodies of rioters were boated across the East River and buried secretly at night. Governor Seymour, who tried to minimize the tragedy, told state legislators that "more than a thousand" civilians, policemen, and soldiers had been slain. Police Superintendent Kennedy, after recovering from his injuries, told G. T. Strong that 1,155 persons had been killed—not counting those smuggled to their graves. Social historian Herbert Asbury wrote that "conservative estimates placed the total at two thousand killed and about eight thousand wounded, a vast majority of whom were rioters." Four days of rioting in New York City produced casualties numbering almost half the total of Americans killed in the American Revolution, just about as many as perished in the War of 1812, and more than all the battle deaths in the Mexican War.[39]

Hostilities only increased after the pogrom. Blacks lost their jobs from fearful employers, were denied work, and faced intensified discrimination and continued segregation. By 1865 New York City's Black population was only 10,000, down 20 percent from the 1860 total.[40]

The mayhem was further endorsed by the "punishments" imposed by the sympathetic judges. Of the estimated 70,000 mobsters, only a few received minor sentences.[41] The draft was not affected by the riots.[42]

Notes

[1] Adrian Cook, *The Armies of the Streets: The New York City Draft Riots of 1863* (Univ. Press of Kentucky, 1974), p. 175.

[2] David M. Ellis et al., *A Short History of New York State* (Ithaca, NY: Cornell Univ. Press in cooperation with the N. Y. State Historical Association, 1957), p. 342; Edward Robb Ellis, *The Epic of New York City* (New York: Coward-McCann, 1966), p. 295.

[3] Ellis, *Epic of New York City*, p. 287.

[4] Philip S. Foner, *Business & Slavery: The New York Merchants & the Irrepressible Conflict* (New York: Russell & Russell, 1968), pp. 1, 4, 6, 7.

[5] Foner, *Business & Slavery* (1968), pp. 1-12; Philip S. Foner, *Business & Slavery: The New York Merchants & the Irrepressible Conflict* (Chapel Hill: Univ. of North Carolina Press, 1941), p. 284; Steven Deyle, "'By farr the most profitable trade': Slave Trading in British Colonial North America," *Slavery and Abolition*, vol. 10, no. 2 (September 1989), p. 112; Leo Hershkowitz, *Tweed's New York: Another Look* (Garden City, NY: Anchor Press/Doubleday, 1977), p. 42.

[6] Foner, *Business & Slavery* (1968), p. 12; Ellis et al., *Short History of New York State*, p. 175.

[7] Foner, *Business & Slavery* (1968), pp. 10, 12, 14; Foner, *Business & Slavery* (1941), p. 284; Ernest A. McKay, *The Civil War and New York City* (Syracuse, NY: Syracuse Univ. Press, 1990), pp. 13, 23.

[8] McKay, *Civil War and New York City*, pp. 23, 41.

[9] Foner, *Business & Slavery* (1968), p. 14.

[10] Kenneth L. Roff, "Brooklyn's Reaction to Black Suffrage in 1860," *Afro-Americans in New York Life and History*, vol. 2, no. 1 (January 1978), p. 33.

[11] Ellis et al., *Short History of New York State*, p. 240; McKay, *Civil War and New York City*, p. 20.

[12] Ellis et al., *Short History of New York State*, p. 238.

[13] Roff, "Brooklyn's Reaction to Black Suffrage," pp. 36-37.

[14] McKay, *Civil War and New York City*, p. 21; Hershkowitz, *Tweed's New York*, p. 42.

[15] Roff, "Brooklyn's Reaction to Black Suffrage," pp. 32, 33, 35, 36.

[16] Ellis et al., *Short History of New York State*, pp. 234, 235, 238; Hershkowitz, *Tweed's New York*, p. 42; McKay, *Civil War and New York City*, p. 27; Dixon Ryan Fox, *The Decline of Aristocracy in the Politics of New York, 1801-1840*, ed. Robert V. Remini (New York: Harper & Row, 1965), p. 270.

[17] McKay, *Civil War and New York City*, pp. 13-14; Ellis et al., *Short History of New York State*, pp. 238, 342.

[18] McKay, *Civil War and New York City*, p. 33; Ellis et al., *Short History of New York State*, p. 242; Foner, *Business & Slavery*, p. 286.

[19] McKay, *Civil War and New York City*, pp. 14, 20, 26, 27, 32-33; Hershkowitz, *Tweed's New York*, pp. 42-43.

[20] McKay, *Civil War and New York City*, p. 14, 18, 19, 25; Hershkowitz, *Tweed's New York*,

notes, continued
   pp. 71-72.
[21]McKay, *Civil War and New York City*, p. 20; Ellis et al., *Short History of New York State*, p. 337.
[22]McKay, *Civil War and New York City*, pp. 12-13, 23; Foner, *Business & Slavery*, p. 14; Ellis et al., *Short History of New York State*, p. 229.
[23]McKay, *Civil War and New York City*, p. 15.
[24]McKay, *Civil War and New York City*, p. 15.
[25]McKay, *Civil War and New York City*, pp. 31-32.
[26]Linda K. Kerber, "Abolitionists and Amalgamators: The New York City Race Riots of 1834," *New York History*, vol. 48, no. 1 (January 1967), p. 28; Iver Bernstein, *The New York City Draft Riots: Their Significance for American Society and Politics in the Age of the Civil War* (New York: Oxford Univ. Press, 1990), p. 5; Federal Writers' Project, *New York Panorama* (New York: Random House, 1938; reprint, 1984), p. 137.
[27]Paul Gilje, *The Road to Mobocracy* (Univ. of North Carolina Press, 1987), p. 143.
[28]Willard A. Heaps, *Riots, U.S.A. 1765-1965* (New York: Seabury Press, 1966), pp. 50-51; Ellis et al., *Short History of New York State*, pp. 336-37; Lawrence Lader, "New York's Bloodiest Week," *American Heritage*, vol. 10, no. 4 (June 1959), pp. 44-45, 48; Bernstein, *The New York City Draft Riots*, pp. 8-10, 27; Cook, *The Armies of the Streets*, p. 174; Leo H. Hirsch, Jr., "The Negro and New York, 1783-1865," *Journal of Negro History*, vol. 16, no. 4 (October 1931), p. 450.
[29]Lader, "New York's Bloodiest Week," p. 48; Ellis, *Epic of New York City*, p. 305.
[30]Heaps, *Riots, U.S.A.*, p. 60; Ellis, *Epic of New York City*, p. 315.
[31]Ellis et al., *Short History of New York State*, p. 337; Heaps, *Riots, U.S.A.*, pp. 52-53.
[32]Heaps, *Riots, U.S.A.*, pp. 53-54; Bob Herbert, "Days of Terror," *New York Times*, 19 October 1997, Op-Ed section, p. 15; Ellis, *Epic of New York City*, p. 307.
[33]Bernstein, *The New York City Draft Riots*, pp. 28-29, 30-31; Hirsch, "The Negro and New York," p. 451; Heaps, *Riots, U.S.A.*, p. 57; Ellis, *Epic of New York City*, pp. 309, 312, 313; Lader, "New York's Bloodiest Week," p. 95.
[34]Heaps, *Riots, U.S.A.*, pp. 58, 59; Bernstein, *The New York City Draft Riots*, p. 28; Hirsch, "The Negro and New York," pp. 452, 453; Ellis, *Epic of New York City*, pp. 305, 315.
[35]Lader, "New York's Bloodiest Week," p. 49; Heaps, *Riots, U.S.A.*, p. 56; Hirsch, "The Negro and New York," p. 451.
[36]Lader, "New York's Bloodiest Week," p. 49; Ellis, *Epic of New York City*, p. 305; Herbert, "Days of Terror," p. 15.
[37]Bernstein, *The New York City Draft Riots*, p. 27; Heaps, *Riots, U.S.A.*, p. 56.
[38] Hirsch, "The Negro and New York," p. 453; Ellis, *Epic of New York City*, p. 315; Heaps, *Riots, U.S.A.*, p. 60; Cook, *Armies of the Streets*, pp. 193-95; Bernstein, *The New York City Draft Riots*, p. 288n; Federal Writers' Project, *New York Panorama*, p. 64.
[39]Ellis, *Epic of New York City*, p. 315.
[40]Cook, *The Armies of the Streets*, p. 175; Rhoda Golden Freeman, *The Free Negro in New York City in the Era before the Civil War* (New York: Garland, 1994), p. 75.
[41]Heaps, *Riots, U.S.A.*, p. 60; Ellis, *Epic of New York City*, p. 316; Hirsch, "The Negro and New York," p. 453.
[42]Lader, "New York's Bloodiest Week," p. 98.

New York Slavery Honored and Remembered

Students of Greater New York attend schools named for people who openly exhibited anti-Black behavior or spewed racist ideologies. Below is just a sampling of New York school names and their relation to the Black race:

John Adams High School

When James Otis declared in 1761 that slavery violated the inalienable rights of man and that all men should be free, Harvard-educated John Adams "shuddered at the doctrine he taught." "It was a doctrine that held terror in it," wrote an Adams biographer. In 1777, Adams teamed with Patriot leader James Warren in opposition to an abolition bill before the Massachusetts House "lest it antagonize their southern allies." After the American Revolution, Adams stated that New York would have joined the British had they not been held in check by the other colonies.[1]

Adams exchanged correspondence with Thomas Jefferson, forecasting the destruction of the Red Indian of North America. Jefferson wrote in 1812: "They will relapse into barbarism and misery, lose numbers by war and want, and we shall be obliged to drive them, with the beasts of the forest, into the Stony mountains." Adams responded: "I believe with you that another conquest of Canada will quiet the Indians forever..."[2]

Simon Baruch Junior High School

Dr. Simon Baruch was a captain in the Confederate Army and a secret member of the *original* Ku Klux Klan. His sons once rummaged through a trunk and found a Confederate uniform, a white hood and a robe of the Knights of the Ku Klux Klan. The clothing belonged to their father, Simon, in whose veins, according to a Baruch biographer, "flowed nothing but Jewish blood." Upon discovering his secret, the boys felt "extravagantly proud of their father," a biographer wrote.[3]

Belmont School

August Belmont, Jewish leader and American representative of the powerful Rothschild banking family, believed the election of Lincoln would be a catastrophe for the nation. He became the national campaign manager for Lincoln's opponent, Steven Douglas, whose rallying cry was "Abolitionism! Niggerism!"[4]

William Cullen Bryant High School

Writer, poet and newspaperman, Bryant harbored deep antipathy toward slavery in some of his writings. He held a deeper antipathy, however, toward Blacks trying to escape it. He ran this advertisement in his newspaper: "TEN DOLLARS REWARD.—Left the City Hotel, on Sunday the 10th instant, a small *Mulatto* Boy, named Marcellus..." When abolitionists challenged his ethics in the matter, he responded thusly:

> ...our advertising columns...are open to the entire community, and will continue to be so, for the publication of notices relating to all transactions which the laws allow....If in fact the boy was a slave...it is most natural for the master to desire to recover him...we shall lay no obstruction in his way....We would remind the *Emancipator* that slave holders...are yet entitled to courteous treatment and fair construction in whatever relates to their personal character and conduct.[5]

After an anti-abolitionist mob of white men rioted in 1833, Bryant said that such violence was to be expected when men as radical as the abolitionists insisted on making public speeches.[6]

Grover Cleveland High School

The 22nd and 24th president of the United States "was no admirer of Black Americans in the mass." Only white

Americans "were capable of appreciating the greatness of the American past and to provide leadership for its future." To Cleveland, Reconstruction—the rebuilding of the South after the Civil War—was a "tragic scar," the product of ignorant Blacks, among others. As governor of New York he twice spoke in favor of segregated schools. Addressing the Southern Education Society in 1903 he said:

> I believe that neither the decree that made the slaves free, nor the enactment that suddenly invested them with the rights of citizenship any more cured them of their racial and slavery-bred imperfections and deficiencies than it changed the color of their skin....I believe that among the nearly nine millions of negroes...there is still a grievous amount of ignorance, a sad amount of viciousness and a tremendous amount of laziness and thriftlessness...[7]

DeWitt Clinton High School

Clinton held several political offices including U.S. senator, mayor of New York City and governor of New York. A descendant of a prominent slaveholding family, he worked for his uncle Governor George Clinton, who owned eight African slaves. Dorothie Bobbe's biography of the man contains this expiatory and typically confusing passage obfuscating the slavery issue:

> At this time his thoughts were also much upon slavery. People said that upper Canada was full of fugitive slaves, and Clinton, an anti-slavery legislator from his youth, went into statistics as usual: "Expenses of bringing up a slave to 18 in Virginia—$468." But he continued to revere a Virginian—his lifelong hero, Thomas Jefferson. "Monticello," he wrote in his diary, "is the Mecca of Virginia."[8]

Benjamin Franklin High School

Boston-born Ben Franklin, the kite-flying colonial icon and America's most illustrious Founding Father mused: "...Why increase the Sons of Africa, by Planting them in America, where we have so fair an opportunity, by excluding Blacks and Tawneys, of increasing the lovely White...?" Though he preferred white indentured slaves in his own household ("We do not like Negro Servants."), Franklin traded Africans from his Philadelphia shop as with any other commodity. He advertised for sale, "a breeding Negro woman about twenty years of age. Can do any household work." Another ad offered "A likely Negro wench about fifteen years old, has had the smallpox." Franklin had no hesitation concerning the buying, selling, brokering and arranging the chattel bondage of African human beings, whom he considered inferior. "Peter," "Jemima," and "George" forfeited their freedom to the Franklins throughout Ben's 30 years as a slaveholder. "Peter" and another slave named "King" even accompanied the Franklins to England where they were forced to "scrub the moss-covered gravestones of the Franklin ancestors."

Franklin's eventual anti-slavery leanings were based not on any moral awakening or newfound love for Blacks, but on the economic inefficiencies of the institution and its discouragement of white immigration and industry. Even when in his latter years he came to the revelation that Blacks were educable as children, grown Blacks, on the other hand, "were still a terrifying people to him."[9]

George Gershwin Junior High School

George Gershwin is the epitome of a culture bandit. He was a white composer whose music took on a decidedly Black flavor upon hearing the music of the great Black blues and jazz greats. His most demeaning work is the oft-performed *Porgy and Bess*, an adaptation of a novel by a Southern white man about the life of a crippled Black beggar (Porgy) and a dope-dealing associate. Gershwin's whiteness alone propelled this debased production to the Broadway stage, while other original works by Black composers were shunned. The great Duke Ellington voiced his outrage: "The times are here to debunk Gershwin's lampblack Negroisms....[N]o Negro could possibly be fooled by *Porgy and Bess*."

Unbelievably, Gershwin, who reportedly used the word "nigger" during rehearsals, was widely considered to be America's "foremost writer of American-Negroid music?" George's brother, lyricist Ira Gershwin, likewise wrote "negroisms" in lyrics such as those for: *I Got Plenty o' Nuttin'*, *Bess, You Is My Woman*, and *There's a Boat Dat's Leavin' Soon for New York*.

European composer and conductor Gunther Schuller said in a 1991 interview: "Of course the blacks lashed out at Gershwin....The blacks have always invented the music. The whites take it over. Then the blacks invent something new."[10]

Samuel Gompers High School

After the Civil War Blacks dominated the skilled trades, particularly in the South. Labor unions were established to force Blacks out of these trades in favor of white immigrants. This era was called the Age of Gompers after the American Federation of Labor (A.F.L.) leader Samuel Gompers. A Jewish immigrant from England, Gompers credits his success to his early training in Hebrew and Talmudic studies at the Jewish Free School in London.[11]

Gompers' A.F.L. refused admittance of Blacks and successfully threw thousands out of work. Gompers promoted and encouraged this racial terrorism by his white union and actually blamed Blacks for being "strikebreakers," whom he threatened with "a race hatred far worse than any ever known." In his public addresses he referred to Blacks as "darkies" and as "superstitious, dull, ignorant, happy-go-lucky, improvident, lazy and, immoral." According to his biographer, Gompers molded the A.F.L. into a true Aryan institution that would affect race and labor relations for more than a century.[12]

Horace Greeley Jr. High School

Like other anti-slavery crusaders of his time, *New York Tribune* publisher Horace Greeley was not so quick to advocate any political rights for the Black man. He, like Lincoln, wanted an end to slavery, but not a beginning to Black freedoms. Greeley believed in the racist "science" that swept white America which "proved" the Black man to be inferior. Blacks, in Greeley's mind, had "natural disabilities...intellectual deficiencies," and were an "inferior race."[13]

Alexander Hamilton High School

Alexander Hamilton grew up as an "illegitimate child" on the slavery-entrenched Caribbean island of Nevis. He held Black slaves throughout his life—a convenient oversight of many historians, who prefer to highlight his anti-slavery utterances. Hamilton was a founder of the New York Manumission Society, though he himself, "never clearly, sincerely, or eloquently denounced slavery in his personal or private works." His inconsistent stance towards slavery, according to a Hamilton biographer, "most likely stemmed from his desire to be accepted in the Manhattan merchant elite, which viewed the ownership of slaves as a status symbol." In fact, the Society rejected a resolution that its members manumit their own slaves. He endorsed the constitutional provision assigning to the Black man just three-fifths of his God-given humanity. Hamilton spoke for his race when he lamented that, "The contempt we have been taught to entertain for the blacks, makes us fancy many things that are founded neither in reason nor experience."[14]

Nathanial Hawthorne Middle School

Hawthorne was born in 1804 of Puritan origin. One of his ancestors sat as a judge at the infamous Salem Witch Trials of 1692. Hawthorne associated with writers like Emerson, Thoreau and Melville but his prolific plume could never address the issues of race and slavery, except once: "On the whole, I find myself rather more of an abolitionist in feeling than in principle."[15]

Patrick Henry Preparatory School

"Give me liberty, or give me death." All 100 of Patrick Henry's Black African slaves desired the same but could never claim freedom in his lifetime. Patrick Henry was a Virginian who believed that Blacks could never attain the necessary skills to be free. He owned plantations in Virginia and Kentucky and was considered one of the largest landowners. Here he advances his solution to the problem of slavery:

> [To] transmit to our descendants, together with our slaves, a pity for their unhappy lot, and an abhorrence of slavery. If we cannot reduce the wished-for reformation to practice, let us treat the unhappy victim with lenity. It is the furthest advance we can make toward justice.[16]

Following these lamentations Henry bought even more slaves and in the Virginia Legislature worked to tighten restrictions on Black movement in the state. Fearful of slave rebellions, Henry voted for the formation of patrols that would periodically terrorize Blacks into the belief that Black liberty in America will, indeed, mean death.[17]

Oliver W. Holmes Junior High School

As a member of the Massachusetts judiciary Holmes handed down 1,300 decisions before being appointed to the Supreme Court in 1902. His record in civil rights cases during his three decades on the Supreme Court "leaned toward support of Southern customs and traditional inbred community attitudes." In the face of state-sponsored terrorism against Blacks in the South Holmes opined: "Political wrongs must be righted by the people and the state itself or by the Congress. Judges must not interfere." Of the all-white jury system, Holmes said "the Court's hands were tied." Holmes called the Blacks who challenged the oppressive debt-slavery system "impulsive people with little intelligence or foresight."

At the end of Holmes's tenure on the bench, a legal scholar concluded that "the black man was not much better off than he had been at the end of the nineteenth century."[18]

Hunter College

Robert Hunter became governor of New York in 1710 and diligently worked to follow the royal orders to increase the trade in African slaves. As an example to other slave owners he sent four of his slaves to a local religious school, which he was convinced would make them better slaves. When, in 1712, the Black man rose up in revolt it was Gov. Hunter's regime that crushed the uprising and administered the brutal punishment that followed. Twenty-one were executed, some were tortured to death, including one who was hanged in chains to die slowly. Governor Hunter regarded this as "the most exemplary punishment inflicted that could be thought of." He soon thereafter supported a bill which discouraged the freeing of Black slaves.

Years later, as an officer in Jamaica, West Indies, fighting rebellious Black slaves called Maroons, Hunter determined that freed Blacks were a threat to white society and that the perpetual servitude of Blacks was inevitable. He, therefore, "willingly approved an act which imposed crippling limitations on the occupations, movements, and activities of freed blacks...."[19]

Andrew Jackson High School

Andrew Jackson owned about 100 Black Africans on his Hermitage Plantation and about 60 at Melton's Bluff Plantation in Alabama. When one got away he placed an ad:

50 DOLLARS REWARD – RAN AWAY from the plantation of Gen. Andrew Jackson...in Franklin County (Ala)...Gilbert, a negro man, about 35 or 40 years of age, very black and fleshy, with a full round face, has a scar on one of his cheeks, but not recollected which....

Jackson cautioned his Alabama overseer, Egbert Harris: "...subordination must be obtained first, and then good treatment."[20]

John Jay College of Criminal Justice

As president of the Society for promoting the Manumission of Slaves, John Jay procured a reputation as "the most articulate advocate of abolition in New York."[21] But in 1798 he admitted that, "I purchase slaves, and manumit them at proper ages, and when their faithful services shall have afforded a reasonable retribution." He, like other members of the Society, held Black Africans in chattel bondage. Jay himself held five. He wrote of his crimes:

> I, John Jay...purchased at Martinico, a negro boy, named Benoit, who has ever since been with me...after the said Benoit shall have served me until the value of his services amount to a moderate compensation for the money expended for him, he should be manumitted; and whereas his services for three years more would, in my opinion, be sufficient for that purpose. Now, know ye, that if the said Benoit shall continue to serve me with a common and reasonable degree of fidelity for three years from the date hereof, he shall ever afterward be a free man....

Jay himself commented hypocritically: "To contend for our own liberty, and to deny that blessing to others, involves an inconsistency not to be excused."[22]

Thomas Jefferson High School

Thomas Jefferson believed Blacks to be as inferior to the white race as the mule is inferior to the horse, created, like the mule, to be the bearer of burdens. To emancipate them would be like turning faithful domestic animals adrift.[23]

Considered "a very bad Farmer," Jefferson held 154 Black slaves on his 10,000 acres in Virginia. All his life, Jefferson closed his eyes to every proof of the growth of slavery. He believed in nothing short of deportation to another hemisphere for Blacks because he anticipated that in the future "our rapid multiplication will...cover the whole northern, if not the southern continent...nor can we contemplate with satisfaction either blot or mixture on the surface." He did, however, acknowledge the crime the colonial "fathers" perpetrated upon future generations of white Americans: "I tremble for my country when I reflect that God is just, and that His justice cannot sleep forever."[24]

Francis Scott Key School

The American Colonization Society was formed in 1816 to facilitate a swift return to Africa for Black people who had been "freed." All of the historical heavyweights signed on to the colonization effort: Henry Clay and James Madison were early leaders, while Gen. Lafayette, James Monroe, *National Anthem* writer Francis Scott Key and many other prominent whites supported the concept. Most Blacks in leadership rejected the "back to Africa" concept, but, for whites, it soon became the most popular and final solution to their Black problem.[25]

Lafayette High School

The French General Marie Joseph Paul Lafayette thought it "unquestionable that differences of intelligence exist among different races of men, and that in this respect some appear far superior to others, but none are on that account the less entitled to the enjoyment of civil and political liberty." Lafayette bought a plantation in South America where he experimented with "freeing the Negroes." He tried to enlist the assistance of his friend the General George Washington to no avail. The French government jailed Lafayette, seized the property and sold the Blacks back into slavery.[26]

James Monroe High School

The fifth U.S. president from 1817-1825, Monroe was governor of Virginia during the so-called Gabriel Conspiracy, where 25 Blacks were slaughtered for actively pursuing their own freedom. Monroe was active in The American

Colonization Society, for he desired that Blacks who had been "freed" be swiftly returned to Africa.[27]

William Penn School

The Quaker founder of Pennsylvania was buying slaves as early as 1655. During the course of his wretched reign, he held Black Africans. One was named "Sampson," whom he traded to a Barbados merchant in exchange for a slave named "Anthony," who was soon replaced by "Jack." Later, Blacks named "Ould Sam," "Virgil," "Sue," "Yaffe" and "Chevalier" would suffer forced enslavement to Penn and his family.

In early 1687, Penn expressed his desire to staff his Pennsbury plantation exclusively with Africans under a white overseer. Said Penn, "It was better they was blacks [sic]." In his home, the Penn women forced two Black women into domestic service, one of whom Penn described as "a most impudent slut."[28]

Theodore Roosevelt High School

Theodore Roosevelt, another great Harvard thinker, believed that Blacks were backward savages who represented an earlier and more primitive species or subspecies of man. "Now as to the Negroes!" he said, "I entirely agree with you that as a race and in the main they are altogether inferior to the whites." Strong white rule was necessary, he thought, to bring them into civilization. Their religions had no ethical basis and the Africans were "ape-like, naked savages, who dwell in the woods and prey on creatures not much wilder or lower than themselves."

The South's greatest crime was not slavery, but bringing so many Africans within America's borders, creating an insoluble problem for whites. Roosevelt opined extensively on the utter inferiority of the Black race and the responsibilities of overlordship which were assigned to the white man. His presidency (1901-1909) saw rampant lynchings and Jim Crow policies but offered only weak condemnation and no Executive action.[29]

John Philip Sousa Junior High School

The "father of the marching band" marched into South Africa during a world tour and had this experience with a Black fan:

> My black friend could not reach my side soon enough; he rushed over to me, and cried, "How d'do, Mr. Sousa! Don' yo' remember me? I'm Jim Nelson f'om Henderson, Nor' Ca'lina!" "How are you, Jim? And what are you doing so far from home?" "Mr. Sousa, I ain't nothin' but a fool nigger. I meets a man in No'folk who says I ought to see the home of my fo'fathers, an' I gets it into my noodle that I gotta see that home o' my fo'fathers. That man gets me a job on a ship comin' over here an' it sailed an' sailed, and fo' de Lord, I'll never do it again! This ain't no place fo' an honest cullud man. These yere Kaffirs do me up at craps. Lord, how they-all can play craps! Now they got all my money an' I ain't got no place to lay my haid. Mr. Sousa, I begs you to take me along with the band. I'll work until I drops in my tracks, only take me, Mr. Sousa, fo' God's sake, take me!" I told him he could come along on the African tour and help with the baggage. He was with us for several weeks, but the story ended like a good many others of similar import; the homesick one fell for a dusky Basuto belle and for all I know, remained in "the land of his fo'fathers" forever after.[30]

Thaddeus Stevens School

Stevens provides still more proof that an "abolitionist" rarely thought any more of Black people than the plantation overseer. He worked "unceasingly" for the employment of Blacks as soldiers in the Civil War. His primary purpose, however, was to strengthen the armed forces and thereby shorten the conflict. In his own words:

> I would put the slaves where they could fight their former masters. If men are to be shot in this war, let it not be our cousins, relatives and friends. Let it be the slaves of those traitors

who have caused the war....The flower of our people are moulding in the swamps of Virginia because we will not employ those who ought to be fighting this battle....And I am to stand here and be told that it will not do to let black men shoot and be shot instead of white men![31]

William H. Taft High School

William Howard Taft was less audible than other U.S. presidents on the issue of Black freedom but his term of 1909-1913 was distinguished by its willing compliance with the oppressive racial status quo. He repeated the sacred white lines of the time, that the southern white man was the only true friend of the negro. To a Black audience he asserted that, "Your race is adapted to be a race of farmers first, last, and for all times." Distrustful of Taft and Roosevelt, Black leaders supported Woodrow Wilson in 1912 whose belief in Ku Klux Klan principles buried the country even more deeply in its racist policies.[32]

Mark Twain School

Probably no American literary figure used the term "nigger" more than did Samuel Clemens, better known as Mark Twain. He grew up in a slaveholding family in the South and fully assimilated the belief in the inferiority of the Black race. He watched his father drag their enslaved African woman "Jennie" outside, as he "bound her hands with a bridle, and whipped her." His trip to New York put him in contact with abolitionists, for whom his disdain was total: "I reckon I had better black my face, for in these Eastern States niggers are considerably better than white people."[33] He had more observations of Manhattan:

> Of all the commodities, manufactures—or whatever you please to call it—in New York, trundle-bed trash—children I mean— take the lead. Why, from Cliff street, up Frankfort to Nassau street, six or seven squares—my road to dinner—I think I could count two hundred brats. Niggers, mulattoes, quadroons,

Chinese, and some the Lord no doubt originally intended to be white, but the dirt on whose faces leaves one uncertain [of] that fact, block up the little, narrow street; and to wade through this mass of human vermin, would raise the ire of the most patient person that ever lived.[34]

Phillis Wheatley School

Phillis Wheatley has been presented as a leader of Black thought of her time. Her poems were deeply religious and have been used to indoctrinate young Black minds. One, entitled "On Being Brought from Africa to America," is as follows:

> Twas mercy brought me from my pagan land,
> Taught my benighted soul to understand
> That there's a God - that there's a Saviour, too:
> Once I redemption neither sought nor knew.
>
> Some view our sable race with scornful eye-
> "Their color is a diabolic dye."
> Remember, Christians, Negroes black as Cain
> May be refined, and join the angelic train.[35]

Wheatley's writing was widely acclaimed in her time and one poem even praised slavemaster George Washington on his appointment to the presidency.[36]

Walt Whitman School

"The nigger, like the Injun, will be eliminated," wrote the poet Whitman, "Someone proves that a superior grade of rats comes and then all the minor rats are cleared out."

As editor of the *Brooklyn Eagle* and the *Brooklyn Times* in the Civil War era, Whitman was no friend of the Black man. Though Whitman was against slavery, his main concern was its effect upon the conditions of white labor. His most racist and popular work is considered to be *Franklin Evans,* which involves sexual fantasies about women of African-American descent.

Whitman "sided ideologically" with president Andrew Johnson (1865-69), a former slave owner who believed whites should continue to hold social dominion over Blacks, whom he considered inferior. "White men alone must manage the South," Johnson told a friend. In Whitman's opinion Blacks were endowed "with about as much intellect and calibre (in the mass) as so many baboons."[37]

Eli Whitney High School

A Yale graduate, Whitney improved upon a mechanical device which removed seeds from cotton, and called it the cotton gin. (The term "gin" is believed to be short for "engine.") This invention, which made cotton manufacturing much more efficient and profitable, is responsible for reviving the slave trade and establishing the Cotton Kingdom. The demand for slaves soared and with the advent of steel-hulled ships, which could carry hundreds more Africans on each voyage, slavery became more entrenched than ever.[38]

John Greenleaf Whittier School

This poet and alleged "abolitionist" is revered as one of America's greatest but in 1831 he wrote to a friend about an incident he witnessed in Hartford:

> We had a frightful row here on Friday night. At about eleven o'clock a band of negroes paraded our streets, knocking down every white man who made his appearance. Eight or ten were injured—and two it is feared will not recover. I hate these negroes, and would think favorably of John Randolph's proposition of shooting them without ceremony. John, if you recollect, is a good marksman, and says he could shoot all his in half an hour, if the other planters would do likewise.[39]

An 1835 letter he wrote to a friend provides evidence of how slavery thrived even among the most ardent "enemies" of Black bondage:

> Do thee know or could thee without much trouble find out, a steady likely colored lad, say 12, or 14 yrs. old, whose parents

would be willing to entrust to my care, as a learner of the 'art and mystery' of farming?–I would do all I could to improve his mind by education and to make him what he ought to be, respectable and virtuous. If thee find such an one, I should be glad to take him to Havll. with me. I, of course, do not want a vicious boy–nor a stupid one.[40]

Places, Landmarks and Streets of New York

Many of the well-known landmarks in New York City and throughout the state have histories of racial oppression or are named for the very same slave merchants and slave holders some people call their "Founding Fathers." Below is an annotated listing of those places.

Avenue of the Americas

Amerigo Vespucci was an Italian associate of Christopher Columbus'. He started to explore the New World shortly after Columbus and it was Vespucci who gave America its name. But Vespucci's adventures have a darker side. In 1498 his crew started to complain that the ships were becoming dangerous to navigate and that they wished to return to their homes in Castile. As Vespucci himself wrote:

Since the men were worn out from having been nearly a year at sea...and the ships were becoming dangerously unseaworthy, the crew cried out that they wished to return to Castile to their homes and that they no longer desired to tempt fortune. Therefore we agreed to seize shiploads of the inhabitants as slaves and to load the ships with them and turn toward Spain....The people were without clothing, timid and ignorant, and we did whatever we wished to do with them....After a long battle, having killed many, we put them to flight, and pursued them to a village, taking about two hundred and fifty prisoners. We burned the village, and returned victorious to the ships with our prisoners, leaving many killed and wounded on their side, while on ours not more than one died, and only twenty-two were wounded.

In Spain, they were "well received, and found a market for our slaves." Thirty-two Red men and women were murdered at sea and the profits from the sale of the surviving victims were divided between the fifty-five "Christian men" who took part in the pillage.[41]

Town of Amherst

No citizens of the British Empire toasted Lord Amherst more sincerely than those of New York in 1760. Both frontier farmers and the Manhattan merchants regarded the redcoats and the royal fleet as their defenders.[42]

In the mid-18th century, Sir Jeffery Amherst was the commander-in-chief of the British Forces in North America. One of his responsibilities in this capacity was to annihilate the Indian population, and it was he who conceived and implemented the strategy to spread smallpox among them. He believed that "the only true method of treating the savages is to keep them in proper subjection and punish, without exception, the transgressors." In a 1763 letter to his colonel, Amherst initiated the first known use of biological warfare in the "New World":

Could it not be contrived to send the smallpox among these disaffected tribes of Indians? We must on this occasion use every stratagem in our power to reduce them.

When he was not engaging in germ warfare, Amherst urged his troops to brutalize the native citizens. He instructed his field commander that when an Indian is captured he is to

...immediately be put to death, their extirpation being the only security for our future safety, and their late treacherous proceedings deserves no better treatment from our hands.

To Amherst, the Indians were

not as a generous enemy, but as the vilest race of beings that ever infested the earth, and whose riddance from it must be esteemed a meritorious act, for the good of mankind. You will therefore take no prisoners, but put to death all that fall into your hands...[43]

Amherst was received as a hero around New England and rewarded in history for these atrocities. A prestigious Massachusetts college and a New York town have been named in his honor.

Central Park

In 1825 the farmland between 83rd and 88th streets and Seventh and Eighth avenues went up for sale. The first purchaser was Andrew Williams, a 25-year-old Black man, who bought three lots for $125. Twenty-four of the 50 parcels were sold to Black families. In just a few years, a Black community they called Seneca Village had developed almost precisely in the middle of the future Central Park, with one Black man, William Matthews, owning almost five acres. As New York custom would dictate, the area soon became known as "Nigger Village." But these "niggers" had developed an instinct for property ownership which helped them to become thirty-nine times more likely to own property as other Black New Yorkers.

New York required that Black voters be landowners, and many of those few who qualified came from Seneca Village. They established schools and churches that helped stabilize the community until mid-19th century when Irish immigrants imposed themselves, making up about 30 percent of the community by 1855.

In 1852 the New York city council recommended the area as the new Central Park. By then, the site was used as a shantytown for 5,000 Irish and German squatters who "lived in huts and ate garbage" and kept 100,000 horses, cows, pigs, goats, chickens, geese, dogs, and cats. Only 20 percent of the park dwellers who owned land, as well as a few others with long-term leases, received compensation for their property.

In 1871 laborers digging up trees at 85th Street and Eighth Avenue uncovered the coffin of "a negro." More than fifty years later, a park gardener discovered an entire graveyard. The *New Yorker* described it as "filled with the bones of tramps and squatters who lived in the Park a hundred or so years ago."[44]

Columbus Circle, Columbia University

Nearly every New York town has an avenue or square named for Christopher Columbus, who discovered that slavery was very profitable; in 1498 his five-ship expedition brought 600 Indians to Spain as slaves. Early on Columbus saw the benefits of slave labor, because before sailing for the New World, he helped to start the Portuguese slave-labor-intensive settlement of San Jorge El Mina in present-day Ghana, formerly known as the Gold Coast.

Even the all-powerful Catholic Church officials were stunned at the blood-soaked trail that Columbus left in his wake. Priest Bartolome de Las Casas, an eyewitness to the carnage, tells us that the Spaniards ranged the Caribbean, "massacring the wretched Indians until in the island of Espanola, which (in 1492) had a population estimated at three millions of people, scarcely three hundred Indians remained to be counted."

[T]he Indians were subjected to the most cruel tortures to compel the disclosure of mines which never existed and the location of gold in streams and fields in which the Almighty had never planted it. Obedience secured no better treatment than sulleness, faithful service had no better reward than that which followed treachery. The meanest Spaniard might violate the family of the most exalted chief, and home had no sanctity in the bestial eyes of the soldier. The courtiers rode proudly through the streets of Isabella and in those of the new Isabella, their horses terrifying the poor Indians while their riders shook their plumed heads and waved their glistening swords. As they rode along their lances were passed into women and children, and no greater pastime was practised by them than wagering as to a cavalier's ability to cleave completely a man with one dexterous blow of his sword. A score would fall before one would drop in the divided parts essential to winning the wager. No card or dice afforded equal sport. Another knight from Spain must sever his victim's head from the shoulder at the first sweep of the sword. Fortunes were lost on the ability of a swordsman to run an Indian through the body at a designated spot. Children were snatched from their mothers' arms and dashed against the rocks as they passed. Other children they threw into the water that their mothers might witness drowning struggles. Babes were snatched from their mothers' breasts, and a brave Spaniard's strength was tested by his ability to tear an infant into two pieces by pulling apart its tiny legs. And the pieces of the babe were then given to the hounds that in their hunting they might be the more eager to catch their prey. The pedigree of the Spanish bloodhound had nothing prouder in its record than the credit of half a thousand dead or mangled Indians. Some natives they hung on gibbets, and it was their reverential custom to gather at a time sufficient victims to hang thirteen in a row, and thus piously to commemorate Christ and the Twelve Apostles. Moloch must have been in the skies.[45]

Erie Canal

The building of the Erie Canal may have had a greater impact on slavery in the South than may have been realized. If the Mississippi River had become the principal artery of commerce for the entire Middle West, then the South would have undoubtedly been a more important commercial center than New York. One historian has said: "It requires no fanciful imagination to conceive that the opening of the Erie Canal was an agency which did more than almost any other to curb the power of slavery."

New York City was not the leading seaport of the United States, nor was New York the Empire State at the time of the Declaration of Independence. Western expansion brought it to first place by 1820; but the building of the Canal contributed greatly to what it is today.[46]

Harlem

About 1637 a Dutchman, named Hendrick De Forest, became the first white man to settle in what is now known as Harlem. By the time Peter Stuyvesant arrived, the Indians had driven the trespassers away. In 1658 Stuyvesant promised that when twenty-five families settled there, he would provide them with a ferry to Long Island and a minister of their own.

They broke ground near the foot of 125th Street and the Harlem River. Apparently Stuyvesant named the community New Haarlem for the town of Haarlem in Holland. The new village was eleven miles from New Amsterdam (at the southern tip of Manhattan Island), the exact distance between Amsterdam and Haarlem in the old country. Enslaved Blacks were immediately committed to constructing a wagon road from New Amsterdam to Harlem.[47]

With Stuyvesant anxious to protect the metropolis, New Harlem ultimately became a garrisoned outpost to New Amsterdam and a barrier against Indian raids—a buffer zone where "half free" Blacks were "given" land.[48]

Lincoln Center; Lincoln Tunnel

Honest Abraham Lincoln never hid his feelings about the Black man: "I agree that he is not my equal in many respects, certainly not in color, perhaps not in moral or intellectual endowment."[49] In his first inaugural address, March 4, 1861, he said:

Apprehension seems to exist among the people of the Southern States, that by the accession of a Republican administration their property and their peace and personal security are to be endangered. There never has been any reasonable cause for such apprehension. Indeed, the most ample evidence to the contrary has all the while existed and been open to their inspection. It is found in nearly all the published speeches of him who now addresses you. I do but quote from one of those speeches when I declare that "I have no purpose, directly or indirectly, to interfere with the institution of slavery in the States where it exists. I believe I have no lawful right to do so, and I have no inclination to do so." Those who nominated and elected me did so with full knowledge that I had made this and many similar declarations, and had never recanted them.[50]

Madison Avenue

James Madison (1751-1836), the Virginia-born fourth president of the United States, was said to oppose slavery but not with enough fervor to "free" any of his family's 118 Black slaves. He considered all Indians to be savages, and his great uncle burned a Black woman at the stake. James placed this notice in a Virginia newspaper in 1786:

> Runaway....A mulatto slave named Anthony about 17 years old but well made, had very light hair and grey eyes;...he has been used to house business and as a waiting servant. Ten Dollars Reward will be given if he be secured so that I get him again....James Madison.

Though he "abhorred" slavery he wanted no Blacks as neighbors and worked on a scheme to export the "freed" slaves back to Africa.[51]

Maimonides Medical Center

Moses Maimonides was a great sage of Judaism whose interpretations of the laws of Moses guided the world's Jews for centuries. His *Guide to the Perplexed* is considered the greatest work of Jewish religious philosophy, but his view of the melanin-rich was somewhat less enlightened:

> [T]he Negroes found in the remote South, and those who resemble them from among them that are with us in these climes [–] The status of those is like that of irrational animals. To my mind they do not have the rank of men, but have among the beings a rank lower than the rank of man but higher than the rank of apes. For they have the external shape and lineaments of

a man and a faculty of discernment that is superior to that of the apes.[52]

Robert Moses State Park

The biography of Robert Moses is called *The Power Broker* for good reason. There is no one in the twentieth century that wielded more power than the largely unknown Robert Moses. Nearly every construction project of note in the city and much of the state was built by permission of Robert Moses. The expressways, the bridges, the parkways, the public housing projects, the playgrounds, the parks with zoos and skating rinks, the golf courses, the beaches and even the dam at Niagra were all built under his authority. No mere politician, or combination of politicians, could match the raw power over New York wielded by Robert Moses.

Moses was also a vicious racist who used his power to oppress Black and Latino people. Moses provides a textbook example of the power of one crazed city planner to create ghettoes, slums and blight along purely racial lines.

Moses threw out of their homes 250,000 persons—more people than lived in Albany or Chattanooga, or in Spokane, Akron, Mobile, Nashville or Sacramento, and according to biographer Robert Caro "a disproportionate share of them were black, Puerto Rican—and poor."

When Moses built housing for poor people, "he built housing bleak, sterile, cheap—expressive of patronizing condescension in every line." And he built it in locations that "contributed to the ghettoization of the city, dividing up the city by color and income."

That is not all. He restricted the use of state parks by poor and lower-middle-class families by limiting access to the parks by rapid transit. He instructed an aide to build the bridges across his new parkways low—too low for buses to pass. Even Governor Roosevelt, the future president, wouldn't interfere when he found out that "Moses was discouraging Negroes from using many of his state parks."

For Negroes, whom he [Moses] considered inherently 'dirty,' there were further measures. Buses needed permits to enter state parks; buses chartered by Negro groups found it very difficult to obtain permits, particularly to Moses' beloved Jones Beach; most were shunted to parks many miles further out on Long Island. And even in these parks, buses carrying Negro groups were shunted to the furthest reaches of the parking areas. And Negroes were discouraged from using 'white' beach areas....

Moses was convinced that Blacks did not like cold water; the temperature at the pool at Jones Beach was deliberately icy to keep Blacks out.

- He poured tens of millions of dollars into creating new parks in New York for whites, but claimed he could do nothing for innercity areas where Blacks lived.

- To discourage "colored" people from using the Thomas Jefferson Pool, Moses, as he had done so successfully at Jones Beach, employed only white lifeguards and attendants.

- Moses deliberately spent $30 million less on Riverside Park in the areas adjacent to the Black and Latino neighborhoods. "He added 132 acres to the parts of the park most likely to be used by white people—but not one acre to the part of the park most likely to be used by black people."

The list of crimes against Blacks and Latinos committed by Robert Moses is actually endless (Caro's Pulitzer Prize-winning book is 1,300 pages), but the fact that the hundreds of thousands of jobs created by the massive construction projects were denied to Blacks and Latinos must be considered one of the greatest racial crimes of the century.[53]

Riker's Island

Judge Richard Riker saw Blacks as separate from the mainstream of the New York community, relegating them to the lowest social level.

When seven-year-old schoolboy Henry Scott was seized as a fugitive slave from his classroom, the kidnappers forcibly brought the terrified child before Richard Riker, the magistrate of New York City. They claimed that the boy was property belonging to white Virginian Clara Haxall. Though they could not produce paperwork substantiating their wicked claim, instead of discharging the case, Riker—reputedly a former slaveholder—postponed the case and sentenced Henry to jail in the interim.[54]

Saint Nicholas Avenue

As a newborn in the fourth century in what is now Turkey, Christmas mascot St. Nicholas was reputed to have "stood upright in his first bath." Blacks entered into the celebration of Christmas within the context of this European folklore. Saint Nicholas' function in the Church was to judge good and evil in children. He would visit children and quiz them on church lessons, rewarding them with candy or gifts, or chastising with sticks or pieces of coal. According to legend, Saint Nicholas was accompanied by a servant named "Black Pete," a "hairy, chained, horned, blackened, devilish monster....clutching a gaping sack in his hairy claws." Black Pete's job was to glare at the children while the saint drilled the youths in Christian verse. Every now and then Black Pete "flashed his enormous canines and leaped, growling, toward the frightened children, threatening to beat them with his rod." Nicholas warned the bad children that Black Pete would stuff transgressors into his sack only to be released at the next Christmas.[55]

Statue of Liberty

Sculptor Frederic Auguste Bartholdi developed an appreciation for Africa during a trip to Egypt where he had been deeply impressed by the pyramids. The first and original U.S. statue of liberty was to be dedicated to the liberation of the Black African slaves recently freed in 1865. The original model had broken chains of slavery at her feet and in her left hand; also "she had a dark Negroid face." This model was simply unacceptable to a nation that only very reluctantly emancipated its African slaves. The broken chains in her left hand were removed and a tablet tucked into her folded arm; "and the Negroid face was altered to look more caucasian."[56]

Wall Street

Wall Street, the financial center of the world, has always been the central trading point in Manhattan. Fearful of Indian and British attacks, Peter Stuyvesant forced his Black captives to clear the dense underbrush and erect a wall which stretched 2,340 feet around the early Dutch settlement. They also cut down brush and trees on what is now Broad Street and planted corn, beans, and other vegetables for their own use. The Dutch Church erected a building at 20 South William Street, to house the enslaved Africans.[57]

A slave market was established at Wall Street in 1711 to be a "place where Negroes and Indians could be bought, sold, or hired." The Wall Street Market comprised various slave markets named after prominent families involved in slave trading, including the Crommelins, Schuylers, Van Zandts, and Waltons.[58] Anne Hartell romanticizes this miserable scene in the expiatory shadings typical of white historians:

> The public slave market at the foot of Wall Street slip was a busy place. Auctioneers shouted prices, urging higher bids in persuasive tones. Buyers—farmers from Long Island or, perhaps, the foremen of well-to-do plantations—wandered through the crowds looking over the coal black newcomers from Africa, who were standing bewildered and dejected on the auction blocks. From the waterfront drifted the noises of sloops unloading,—the chants of negro stevedores, the rumble of molasses kegs rolling down a gangplank, a sailor's fight before a tavern. And the singing of the anvil drifted up from the forge on the nearby Strand of the East River. In such an atmosphere the Africans found their new masters.[59]

George Washington Bridge

America's father, George Washington, was one of the largest slave owners in American history. His home state of Virginia was the prime breeder of Black people for the domestic slave trade and at one point the state exported 6,000 Black people annually—their biggest "cash crop." In 1786 Washington held 216 Black Africans—116 workers, 92 children and 8 infirm. This unusually high number of children who were unable to work the plantation indicates that George was heavily involved in the breeding of Black people for the slave trade. Washington gave them such names as:

Sall Brass	Hercules	Winny
Breechy	Giles	Sucky
Suck	Paris-boy	Flukey
Lame Alice	Doll	Suck Bass
Virgin	Cook Jack	House Sall
Jupiter	Sambo	Caesar
Dorcas	Opey	Cupid

From his birth to his death (and beyond) Washington was a slaveholder. He controlled 317 Black human beings at his death in 1799.[60]

Notes

[1]Otis was considered to be insane from 1769 on. See George F. Willison, *Saints and Strangers* (New York, 1945), p. 480n; Robert C. Twombly, "Black Resistance to Slavery in Massachusetts," *Insights and Parallels: Problems and Issues of American Social History* (Minneapolis: Burgess, 1973), ed. William L. O'Neill, p. 12; Catherine Drinker Bowen, *John Adams and the American Revolution* (Boston: Little, Brown, 1950), pp. 217, 567; Samuel Adams Drake, *Old Landmarks and Historic Personages of Boston* (Boston: Little, Brown, 1900), p. 60.

[2]Lester J. Cappon, ed., *The Adams-Jefferson Letters*, vol. 2 (Chapel Hill: Univ. of North Carolina Press, 1959), pp. 307-308, 310-11.

[3]Harry Simonhoff, *Jewish Participants in the Civil War* (New York: Arco, 1963), p. 225; See the discussion of, and justification for, Baruch's Klan membership, in Margaret L. Coit, *Mr. Baruch* (Boston: Houghton Mifflin, 1957), pp. 1-32; Carter Field, *Bernard Baruch: Park Bench Statesman* (New York: McGraw-Hill, 1944), p. 2; James Grant, *Bernard M. Baruch: The Adventures of a Wall Street Legend* (New York: Simon & Schuster, 1983), p. 21.

notes, continued

[4]Ernest A. McKay, *The Civil War and New York City* (Syracuse, NY: Syracuse Univ. Press, 1990), pp. 18, 19; William Harlan Hale, *Horace Greeley: Voice of the People* (New York: Harper, 1950), p. 162.

[5]William Cullen Bryant II, *Power for Sanity: Selected Editorials of William Cullen Bryant, 1829-1861* (New York: Fordham Univ. Press, 1994), pp. 52-53.

[6]Lorman Ratner, *Powder Keg: Northern Opposition to the Antislavery Movement, 1831-1840* (New York: Basic Books, 1968), p. 84

[7]Richard E. Welch, *The Presidencies of Grover Cleveland* (Univ. Press of Kansas, 1988), pp. 68-69.

[8]Shane White, *Somewhat More Independent: The End of Slavery in New York City, 1770-1810* (Athens, Georgia: Univ. of Georgia Press, 1991), p. 10; Dorothie Bobbe, *De Witt Clinton* (New York: Minton, Balch, 1933), p. 256.

[9]Claude-Anne Lopez, *The Private Franklin* (New York: W.W. Norton, 1975), pp. 291-302; Carl Van Doren, *Benjamin Franklin* (New York: Viking Press, 1938), pp. 128-29.

[10]Charles Schwartz, *Gershwin: His Life and Music* (Indianapolis: Bobbs-Merrill, 1973), pp. 139, 243-45, 261-62, 264; Joan Peyser, *The Memory of All That: The Life of George Gershwin* (New York: Simon & Schuster, 1993), pp. 235, 237, 251.

[11]Lucian B. Gatewood, "The Black Artisan in the U.S., 1890-1930," *The Review of Black Political Economy*, vol. 5, no. 1 (1974), pp. 20-21, 23, 24-25, 27, 31, 32-33; Samuel Gompers, *Seventy Years of Life and Labor: An Autobiography*, vol. 1 (New York: E.P. Dutton, 1925), pp. 6-7.

[12]Marc Karson and Ronald Radosh, "The American Federation of Labor and the Negro Worker, 1894-1949," *The Negro and the American Labor Movement*, ed. Julius Jacobson (Garden City, NY: Anchor Books/Doubleday, 1968), pp. 155, 158-59; Herbert Shapiro, review of *Samuel Gompers, A Biography*, by Bernard Mandel, *Journal of Negro History*, vol. 50, no. 4 (October 1965), pp. 283-84.

[13]Ralph Ray Fahrney, *Horace Greeley and the* Tribune *in the Civil War* (Cedar Rapids, Iowa: Torch Press, 1936), p. 111; Jeter Allen Isely, *Horace Greeley and the Republican Party, 1853-1861: A Study of the* New York Tribune (Princeton: Princeton Univ. Press, 1947), p. 33.

[14]Rob N. Weston, "Alexander Hamilton and the Abolition of Slavery in New York, *Afro-Americans in New York Life and History*," vol. 18, no. 1 (January 1994), pp. 31-32, 34-35; Nathaniel Weyl and William Marina, *American Statesmen on Slavery and the Negro* (New Rochelle: Arlington House, 1971), pp. 57-63.

[15]Claude M. Simpson, ed., *The American Notebooks*, vol. 8, *Nathaniel Hawthorne* (Ohio State Univ. Press, 1972), p. 112.

[16]Richard R. Beeman, *Patrick Henry: A Biography* (New York: McGraw Hill, 1974), pp. 95-97.

[17]Robert Douthat Meade, *Patrick Henry: Practical Revolutionary* (Philadelphia: J.B. Lippincott, 1969), pp. 312, 421, 437; Moses Coit Tyler, *Patrick Henry* (New Rochelle, NY, 1970), p. 388.

[18]Liva Baker, *The Justice from Beacon Hill: The Life and Times of Oliver Wendell Holmes* (New York: HarperCollins Publishers, 1991), pp. 386, 388, 471-74, 598.

[19]Sheldon S. Cohen, "Elias Neau, Instructor to New York's Slaves," *The New-York Historical Society Quarterly*, vol. 55, no. 1 (January 1971), pp. 18, 20; Roi Ottley and William J. Weatherby, eds., *The Negro in New York: An Informal Social History* (Dobbs

notes, continued

Ferry, NY: Oceana Publications, 1967), p. 23; Thomas Joseph Davis, "Slavery in Colonial New York City" (Ph.D. diss., Columbia Univ., 1974), p. 114; Mary Lou Lustig, *Robert Hunter, 1666-1734: New York's Augustan Statesman* (Syracuse, NY: Syracuse Univ. Press, 1983), pp. 194-95.

[20]Marquis James, *Andrew Jackson: Portrait of a President* (New York, 1937), pp. 29-31.

[21]Edgar J. McManus, "Antislavery Legislation in New York," *Journal of Negro History* 46, no. 4 (October 1961), p. 207.

[22]William Jay, *The Life of John Jay*, vol. 1 (New York, 1833), pp. 230, 231, 235.

[23]Helen Nicolay, *Our Capital on the Potomac* (New York, 1924), p. 343; Margaret Bailey Tinkcom, "Caviar along the Potomac: Sir Augustus John Foster's 'Notes on the United States,' 1804-1812," *William and Mary Quarterly* (January 1951), vol. 8, no. 1, p. 103.

[24]Tinkcom, "Caviar along the Potomac," p. 102; Sarah N. Randolph, *The Domestic Life of Jefferson* (Univ. Press of Virginia, 1978), pp. 228-29; Weyl and Marina, *American Statesmen*, p. 84; David L. Lewis, *District of Columbia: A Bicentennial History* (New York: W.W. Norton, 1976), pp. 43-44.

[25]Clay owned 50 slaves on his Kentucky plantation. Helen Nicolay, *Our Capital on the Potomac*, p. 343; Constance McLaughlin Green, *The Secret City: A History of Race Relations in the Nation's Capital* (New Jersey: Princeton Univ. Press, 1967), pp. 22-23; Gibbs Myers, "Pioneers in the Federal Area," *Records of the Columbia Historical Society*, vol. 44-45 (1944), p. 143.

[26]Weyl and Marina, *American Statesmen*, pp. 40-42.

[27]Weyl and Marina, *American Statesmen*, pp. 109-10; Nicolay, *Our Capital on the Potomac*, p. 343; Green, *The Secret City*, p. 23.

[28]Harry Emerson Wildes, *William Penn* (New York: Macmillan, 1974), pp. 322-26.

[29]Weyl and Marina, *American Statesmen*, pp. 299-304, 315-18.

[30]John Philip Sousa, *Marching Along: Recollections of Men, Women and Music* (Boston: Hale, Cushman & Flint, 1928), p. 267.

[31]Ralph Korngold, *Thaddeus Stevens: A Being Darkly Wise and Rudely Great* (New York: Harcourt, Brace, 1955), pp. 204-205.

[32]Rayford W. Logan, *The Negro in the United States* (1957), pp. 65-68.

[33]Andrew Jay Hoffman, *Inventing Mark Twain: The Lives of Samuel Langhorne Clemens* (New York: William Morrow, 1997), pp. 6, 35.

[34]Robert H. Hirst et al., eds., *Mark Twain's Letters*, vol. 1, *1853-1866* (Berkeley & Los Angeles: Univ. of California Press, 1988), p. 10.

[35]John Daniels, *In Freedoms Birthplace* (Houghton Mifflin, 1914; reprint, Negro Universities Press, 1968), pp. 20-21.

[36]Benjamin Quarles, *The Negro in the American Revolution* (Chapel Hill: Univ. of North Carolina Press, 1961), pp. 45-46.

[37]Larry D. Griffin, review of *Whitman, Slavery, and the Emergence of Leaves of Grass*, by Martin Klammer, *Walt Whitman Quarterly Review*, vol. 12, no. 4 (spring 1995), pp. 261-62; David S. Reynolds, *Walt Whitman's America: A Cultural Biography* (New York: Knopf, 1995), pp. 464-72.

[38]Constance McLaughlin Green, *Eli Whitney and the Birth of American Technology*, ed. Oscar Handlin (Boston: Little, Brown, 1956), pp. 47, 191; Jeannette Mirsky and Allan Nevins, *The World of Eli Whitney* (New York: Macmillan, 1952), p. 289.

[39]John B. Pickard, ed., *The Letters of John Greenleaf Whittier*, vol. 1, *1828-1845* (Cambridge,

notes, continued

MA: Harvard Univ. Press, 1975), pp. 57-58.

[40]Pickard, *The Letters of John Greenleaf Whittier*, p. 163.

[41]See Frederick J. Pohl, *Amerigo Vespucci Pilot Major* (New York: Columbia Univ. Press, 1944); Germain Arciniegas, *Amerigo and the New World*, trans. Harriet DeOnis (New York: Knopf, 1955); Stefan Zweig, *Amerigo, A Comedy of Errors in History* (New York: Vilening Press, 1942); Charles Edwards Lester and Andrew Foster, *Life and Voyages of Americus Vespucius* (New York: Baker & Scribner, 1846).

[42]David M. Ellis et al., *A Short History of New York State* (Ithaca, NY: Cornell Univ. Press in cooperation with the N. Y. State Historical Association, 1957), pp. 58-59.

[43]See Alvin M. Josephy, Jr., *The Patriot Chiefs: A Chronicle of American Indian Resistance* (New York: Viking Press, 1958); Francis Parkman, *The Conspiracy of Pontiac* (New York, 1962).

[44]Roy Rosenzweig and Elizabeth Blackmar, *The Park and the People: A History of Central Park* (Ithaca, NY: Cornell Univ. Press, 1992), pp. 65-73, 88-89; Edward Robb Ellis, *The Epic of New York City* (New York: Coward-McCann, 1966), p. 271.

[45]Wilford, *The Mysterious History of Columbus*, pp. 178-79; Sir Arthur Helps, *The Spanish Conquest in America*, vol. 1 (New York, 1900), pp. 113-14; Eric Rosenthal, *Gold! Gold! Gold!* (Johannesburg: Macmillan, 1970), p. 71; See Bartolome de Las Casas, *History of the Indies*, trans. & ed. Andrée Collard (New York: Harper & Row, 1971).

[46]Peter Nelson, "Influence of the Erie Canal in the Development of the Nation," *Rochester Historical Society*, vol. 8 (1929), pp. 262-63.

[47]Ellis, *Epic of New York City*, p. 52; Joyce D. Goodfriend, "Burghers and Blacks: The Evolution of a Slave Society at New Amsterdam," *New York History*, vol. 59 (April 1978), pp. 130-31.

[48]Edwin Olson, "Negro Slavery in New York, 1626-1827" (Ph.D. thesis, New York Univ., 1938), p. 25n; James Riker, *Harlem: Its Origins and Early Annals* (Upper Saddle River, NJ: Literature House/Gregg Press, 1970), p. 202.

[49]Albert E. Pillsbury, *Lincoln and Slavery* (Boston & New York: Houghton Mifflin, 1913), p. 33.

[50]Page Milburn, "The Emancipation of the Slaves in the District of Columbia," *Records of the Columbia Historical Society*, vol. 16 (1913), pp. 113-14.

[51]Ralph Ketcham, *James Madison: A Biography* (New York: Macmillan, 1971), pp. 374-75, 625-30. See also Sydney Howard Gay, *James Madison* (Boston, 1898), p. 109.

[52]Moses Maimonides, *The Guide to the Perplexed*, Book III, translated by Shlomo Pines (Univ. of Chicago Press, 1963), pp. 618-19. See another translation in Israel Shahak, *Jewish History, Jewish Religion: The Weight of Three Thousand Years* (London: Pluto Press, 1994), p. 25.

[53]Robert A. Caro, *The Power Broker: Robert Moses and the Fall of New York* (New York: Knopf, 1974), pp. 6-9, 19-20, 242, 318-19, 492-93, 512-14, 532-33, 557, 736. See how another historian attempts to apologize for the Moses record: Cleveland Rodgers, *Robert Moses: Builder for Democracy* (New York: Henry Holt, 1952), pp. 213-17.

[54]Paul Gilje, *The Road to Mobocracy* (Univ. of North Carolina Press, 1987), p. 169; Lawrence B. Goodheart, "'The Chronicles of Kidnapping in New York': Resistance to the Fugitive Slave Law, 1834-1835," *Afro-Americans in New York Life and History*, vol. 8, no. 1 (January 1984), p. 8.

[55]Phyllis Siefker, *Santa Claus, Last of the Wild Men: The Origins and Evolution of Saint*

notes, continued

Nicholas (Jefferson, N. Carolina: McFarland, 1997), pp. 7-15.

[56]"The Liberty Legend," *New York Times Magazine*, 18 May 1986; *New York Post*, 17 June 1986; Jack Felder, "This Miss Liberty was Modeled on Racism" (Dept. of Africana Studies, City College of New York, photocopy).

[57]Charles E. Corwin, "Efforts of the Dutch Colonial Pastors for the Conversion of the Negroes," *Journal of the Presbyterian Historical Society*, vol. 12, no. 7 (April 1927), p. 426; Ellis, *Epic of New York City*, p. 59; Ellis et al., *Short History of New York State*, p. 20.

[58]Ottley and Weatherby, *The Negro in New York*, p. 19; Joyce D. Goodfriend, *Before the Melting Pot: Society and Culture in Colonial New York City, 1664-1730* (Princeton, NJ: Princeton Univ. Press, 1992), p. 121; Davis, "Slavery in Colonial New York City," p. 180; Kenneth Jackson, ed., *Encyclopedia of New York City* (Yale Univ. Press, 1995), p. 1076; Olson, "Negro Slavery in New York," p. 70.

[59]Anne Hartell, "Slavery on Long Island," *Nassau County Historical Journal*, vol. 6, no. 2 (fall 1943), p. 56. Hartell suggests that the Africans were *looking for* and indeed *wanting* masters, rather than brutally being forced to an auction block for permanent chattel bondage.

[60]Frederic Bancroft, *Slave Trading in the Old South* (New York, 1931), pp. 67-87; "George Washington," *American History Illustrated*, February 1985, p. 16; "Diary of George Washington," *Publications of The Colonial Society of Massachusetts*, April 1902, pp. 358-64.

New York Slave Owners

It is known that all wealthy New York whites owned slaves, some as many as fifty. Even people of moderate means had three to six African captives in their households, "whom they regarded as impersonally as they did chairs and tables."[1]

The following is an *abbreviated* list of New York slave owners and traders based in part on many of the sources herein cited. It is provided as a genealogical public service to the reader who may be seeking compensation for the unending toil of their New York foreparents. What may appear to be repetitions or slight name variations or misspellings appear in the original documents. The practice of bequeathing Black Africans from one generation of kidnappers to the next may account for some of the repeating surnames. There were, of course, hundreds more:

Mr. Abeel	John Allison	Gilbert Aspinwall	Roger Baker
Garrit B. Abeel	Robert Allison	John Aspinwall	John Ball
John N. Abeel	Josheph Alson	Margaret Aspinwall	Christopher Bancker
Jno. Abrams	Richard Alson	Jno. Auboyneau	Gerrit Bancker
Jon. Abrams	Richard Alsop	Jno. Auboyneaux	Rachel Banister
Henry Ackerman	Richard Alsup	Douwe Aukes	Samuel Banister
Jane Adams	John Amerman	Isaac Auld	Christopher Banker
John G. Adams	Joshua Amy	Jonathan Austen	John Banker
Jacamiah Akerly	John Anderson	Daniel Austin	David Banks
William Alburtis	William Anderson	Mary Avice	Samuel Banks
Derick Alderson	Barent Andriese	Susan Aycrigg	Peter Barberie
James Alexander	Richard Annely	James Aymar	John Barberie
Mary Alexander	John Anten	Mr. Bachan	Peter Barberie
Dav. Algeo	Nicholas N. Anthony	Hendreck Backmen	Edward Bardin
Jos. Alison	George Arcularius	Hendrick Backmen	Micael Bargan
Elizabeth Allair	Charles Arding	Ebenezer Backus	Derk Bargay
Peter Allaire	Mary Armour	John B. Bacque	John Bargay
Samwell Allburtes	Samuel Armour	Daniel Baehr	Saartje Barkeloo
Abraham Allen	Edward Arnold	Benjamin Bailey	Daniel Barker
John Allen	Isaac Arnold	Theodorus Bailey	William Barker
Nehemiah Allen	Robert Arter	Nathaniel Baily	Robert Barnes
Pamela Allen	Elbert Artsea	Calvin Baker	Thos. Barnes
Stephen Allen	Gilbert Ash	David Baker	Wm. Barnes
David Allgoe	Robert Ash	James Baker	Joshua Barns

---

[1] Ellis, *Epic of New York City*, p. 112.

Thomas Barns
Undrill Barns
Vndrill Barns
James Barrow
Anthony Barto
Bassill Barto
Theophilus Barto
Delia Bartow
Jno. Bassett
Abraham Bates
Soloman Bates
Thomas Batts
Jacob Baurhyte
Augustin Baxter
Philip Baxter
Nicholas Bayard
Robert Bayard
Sam'l Bayard
St. Bayard
St'n Bayard
Steph'n Bayard
Stephen N. Bayard
William Bayard
Thos. Bayeaux
Thos. Bayeaux Jr.
Mr. Bayeur
Thomas Bayles
Nicolas Baylie
Thomas Beavan
Hendrick Beckman
Marte Beckman
Israel Bedell
Jerm Bedell
John Bedell
Samuel Beebee
Thomas Beeckman
Willem Beeckman
Charles Beekman
Gerard G. Beekman
Gerardus Beekman
Gerrard Beekman
Henry Beekman
James Beekman
John Beekman
Wm. Beekman
William Pitt Beers
Joseph Begel
Thomas Behenna
Charles Belcour
Andrew Bell
Beniwell
Jacob Bennet
Jacob W. Bennet
Winant Bennet
George Bennett
Jacob Bennett
Margerit Bennin
Egbert Benson
Robert Benson
David Berdan
Garret Bergen

Jacob Bergen
Eloy Berger
Peter Bernson
Cornelius Berrian
James Berrian
Richard P. Berrian
Richard Berry
William Berry
Elizabeth Bertan
L. Bertie
Dannel Bets
Joseph Bets
Richard Bets
Whillem Bets
Abraham Bevier
Jacobus Bevier
Levis Bevier
Philip Bevier
Samuel Bevier
Abraham D. Bevois
John Biggs
John Bingham
Benjamin Birdsall
Daniel Birdsall
Josh: Birdsall
Oliver Birdsall
Benjamin Birdsell
John Blacklock
Daniel Blackly
Jacob Blackwell
Joseph Blackwell
Lydia Blackwell
Mary Blackwell
Matthys Blanjan
Johannes Blauveldt
Garret Blauvelt
Jacob Blauvelt
John A. Blauvelt
James L. Bleecker
Leonard Bleecker
Richard Blidenburge
Gilbert Blomer
Abraham Bloodgood
Joseph Bloodgood
Abraham Bloom
Bernardis Bloom
Reuben Bloomer
Jury Bloue
Justus Boch
Mme. Bocquet-fressinet
Gerret Boerem
Jan Boerem
Karel Boerem
Nich's. Boerum
Tuenes Bogaert
Benjamin Bogardus
Egbert Bogardus
Evert Bogardus
Nickolas Bogardus
Petrus Bogardus
Abraham O. Bogart

Henry I. Bogart
Isaac H. Bogart
Johannes Bogart
Joseph O. Bogart
Marten Bogart
Cornelius I. Bogert
Elizabeth Bogert
Helena Bogert
Jacobus Bogert
Isaac Bolding
James Bolt
Simon Bonane
Abraham Bond
Mr. Bone
James Bonney
Ezekiel Bonyot
Simon Booram
Nicolaes Boot
Mary Jane Borduzat
Isack Borgow
Peter Borgow
Isack Borgow Jr.
Sarah Borrell
Jasp'r Bosch
Justus Bosch
Sarah Bostwick
Elias Boudinot
Jacob Bound
Thomas Bound
Sam'l Bourdet
John Bout
Samuel Bouton
George Bowen
John Bowne
Obadiah Bowne
Samuel Boyd
Samuel Boyd, Esq.
Jos. Boyd'n
Samuel Bradhurst
Jno. Bradick
Margaret Bradish
Daniel Braine
William Bramebosch
Widow Brandt
John Brazier
Madam Brett
William Brett
Abrm Brewer
Nathaniel Brewster
Samuel Brewster
Alexander Briant Jr.
Underhill Bridd
Samuel Bridge
Charles Bridges
James Briggs
Walter Brigs
Lambert Brinck
Abraham Brinckerhoff
Cornelious Brink
Henderick Brink
Jacob Brink

Hendrick Brinkerhoff
Sebe Brinkerhoff
Georg Brinkkerhouf
Tunus Brinkkerhouf
F. Brinley
Amos Broad
Sam'el Broadhurst
Charles Brodhad
Daniel Brodhead
Jacob Brodhead
Wessel Brodhead
Isaac Bronson
Anne Brooks
Catharine Brooks
Dr. Brouner
Benjaman Brown
Capt. Brown
Gilbert Brown
Hannah Brown
Hasechiah Brown
Jno. Brown
John Brown
Jon. Brown
Jonethan Brown
Joshua Brown
Mary Brown
Robt. Brown
Samuell Brown
Thomas Brown
Benjaman Brown Jr.
Nehemiah Brown Jr.
John Browne
Robert Browne
Thos. Browne
William Browne
Charles Brownne
Judith Bruce
Robert L. Bruce
Jery Bruer
David Bruester
Jacob Bruington
Joseph Brundig
Israel Brush
Ebenezer Brush
Robert Brush
Samuel Brush
Thomas Brush
Cornelius Bruyn
Jacobus Bruyn
Severyn Bruyn
Augustin Bryan
Mary Bryant
Thomas Buckley
Joseph Bueno
William Bull
William Bullock
Thomas Bunce
Abel Buntier
George Burchill
Daniel Burdett
Elias Burger

Harmanus Burger
Martin Burger
Daniel Burger Sr.
Samuel Burgess
David Burhans
Abrm. Burhans
Jacob Burhans
John Burhans
Margareit Burhans
David Burhans Jr.
John Burhans Jr.
Edw'd Burling
Jas. Burling
Aaron Burr
Jonathan Burrell
Thomas Burroughs Jr.
Sarah Burrows
Benjaman Burt
Peter A. Burtis
Henry Bush
Jesper Bush
Justis Bush
Just's Bush
William Bush
Abreham Bust
Abram Butler
Abram Buttler
Peter Byard
Stephen Byard
Thomas Byowan
Joseph Cale
Littellier Cambie
Cloacha Campbell
Dud. Campbell
Samuel Campbell
Abraham Cannon
Andrew Cannon
David Cannon
John Cannon
Peter Cannon
Matthew Cantine
Peter Cantine
Peter Cantine Jr.
Gorge Car
Jesse Carl
Timothy Carl Jr.
Timothy Carle Sr.
Jno Carman
Phineas Carman
Silas Carman
Thos. Carman
Benj: Carmon
Thomas Carpender
Thomas Carpender Jr.
Benjamin Carpenter
John Carpenter
Nathaniel Carpenter
Thomas Carpenter
Thorne Carpenter

Timothy Carpenter
Gideon Carstang
Jacob Casperse
Mr. Catale
Jean Caverly
William Chace
Abrm. Gaasbeck Chambers
John Chambers
Thomas Champenois
Raynal Chardonnay
Mary Charlton
Thomas Charnock
Isaac Chauncey
Francis Child
Albert Chrystie
James Chrystie
Mary Chrystie
Thomas Chrystie
Henry Chuyler
Elias Clap
Cornelius Clapper
Ann Clark
George Clark
Jeremiah Clark
Scott Lawrence Clark
George Clarke
Godney Clarke
James B. Clarke
John Clarke
Lt. Gov. Clarke
Peter Clarke
Matthew Clarkeson
Charles Clarkson
David Clarkson
Matt. Clarkson
Matth'w Clarkson
Widow Clarkson
Isaac Clawson
Charles Clinton
De Witt Clinton
George Clinton
Elizabeth Clock
Marten Clock
Peter Clous
Johannes Clute
James Cochran
John Cochran
Daniel Cock
Deborah Cock
Henry Cock
Hezekias Cock
John Cock
Oliver Cock
James Coden
Ja's Coden
Christopher Codwise
George Codwise
John Coe
Henry Coerteen

John Coffin
Samuel Myers Cohen
Solomon Myers Cohen
Cadwallader Colden
David Colden
Daniel Coles
John B. Coles
Joseph Coles
Robert Coles
Wright Coles
John Combs
Mr. Conrads Comfort
Jacob Concklin
Silas Condit
Epenetus Conklin
Joseph Conklin
Platt Conklin
John Conley
Peter Conselye
Isaac Contine
Moses Contyn
Robert Coo
Mr. Cook
Cornelius Cool
John Cooley
John Cooper
Joseph Cooper
Simon Cooper
John Corey
Fred. Corland
Lord Cornbury
Barth Cornell
Cornelia Cornell
Elijah Cornell
Hannah Cornell
Jacobus Cornell
John Cornell
Joseph Cornell
Josheph Cornell
Richard Cornell
Thos. Cornell
William Cornell
Richard Cornell Jr.
Aspinwall Cornwall
John Cornwell
Whitead Cornwell
Cristeiaen Corssen
Jacob Corssen Jr.
Jacob Corssen Sr.
Jaques Cortelyou
Pieter Cortelyou
Jaques Cortelyou Jr.
Phil. Cortland
Phil Cortlandt
Daniel Corwin
Henry Courteen [also spelled Coerteen or Coertens]
Garrat Couzine
Jacob Cowenhoven

John Cowenhoven
Nicholas R. Cowenhoven
Gerret Cozyn
John Craig
Phebe Crane
Casper Crapster
Absalom Crawford
John Crawford
Antonie Crispel
Jan Crispell
Johannis Crispell
Petrus Crispell
John Crispell Jr.
Abraham Crocheron
Jacob Crocheron
John Crocheron
Cherls Crock
Cattrienna Croeck
Jo Croffert
Chas. Cromlin
Chas. Cromline
Crommelin
John Croocke
John Crooke
Mos. Crooker
Robert Crooker
William Crooker
Hendrick Croom
Wm. Crow
Cruger
Henry Cruger
Jno. Cruger
Telem Cruger
Tulem Cruger
Jno. Cruger Jr.
Jon. Cruger Jr.
Elizabeth Crum
Chas. Crumline
Cornelius Cruse
Henry Cruse
Garret Crussen
Cornelius Crygier
David A. Cumming
Richard Cunningham
John Cure
Curtis
Joseph Curtis
Richard Cussens (a.k.a. Cousens)
Henry Cuyler
Henry Cuyler Jr. & Sr.
John Dain
James Darcey
Jas. Darcey
James Darcy
Jas. Darcy
Robert Darkins
John Darugrand
John B. Dash

Newburry Davenport
David Davis
Frederick Davis
Joel Davis
John Davis
Richard Davis
Ellixander Davorson
Frederick Davoue
Aigar De
Samuel Deall
Joseph Dean
Richard Dean
Kesia Deane
James Dearin
John De Baan
Jacobus Debavois
Johanis Debavois
Joost Debavois
Karel Debavois
George De Bevoice
Jacob De Bevoice
Sam: De Bevoice
John De Bevoyce
Isaac Deccar
John Deceer
Jacob Decker
John Decker
Marities Decker
John de Decker
Jacobus Degraew
George De Grass
Margaret Degroodt
John de Honeur
John [or Johannes] Dehonneur
Cornel Dekay
Georg Dekay
Helena Dekey
Peter De Lacey
John Delafield
Abraham Delameter
Marten Delameter
Jacobus Delametter
Johannis De Lametter
William de la Montagne
James DeLancey
John DeLancey
Oliver DeLancey
Peter Delancey
Stephen De Lancey
Steph. DeLancey
Stephen Delancey
James De Lancy
Stephen Delancy
James K. Delaplaine
Abr. Delmena
Daniel S. Demarest
Thomas Demarrest
Nicholas Demyer [De Myer]
Christifor Dene
Deneys Deneys
Isaac Denham

Thomas Denis
William Denning
Jeronimus Dense
Nehemiah Denton
Isaac Denyce
Corn Depetyr
Isaac Depetyr
Abr. Depeyst Jr.
Abr'm De Peyster
Anna De Peyster
Col. Depeyster
Cornelius DePeyster
Frederick DePeyster
Coll. Depeyter
Barnit De Pue
Margaret Derienier
Henry Dering [or Deering]
Sylvester Dering
Thomas Dering
John Derring
Thomas Derring
Nicholas De Sille
Simja De Torres
Richard Devenport
Samuel Devenport
Jan de Vries
John De Wint
Johannes DeWit
Peak Dewit
Peter De Wit
Andries DeWitt
Johannes Dewitt
Peter DeWitt
Tjerck Dewitt
Anthony Dey
John Lopes Dias
Townsend Dickensen
Henry Dickenson
Gilchrist Dickinson
Mr. DiCromelin
Robert Dikensen
D. C. Dinnies
Anne Disbro
Hanah Disbrow
Peter Dispinou
John Ditmars
Laurens Ditmars
Douwe Ditmarss
Johannes Ditmarss
David Dixon
Henry Dodge
Levi Dodge
Phoebe Dodge
James Dole
Mr. Dole
William Dondij
Thomas Dongan
James Dorcey
Isaac Doty
Charles Doughty
John Doughty

Volkert A. Douw
Eleanor Dowllensd
Beniaman Downing
Benjamin Downing
Dennis Downing
Abraham Doyo
Christiaan Doyo
Peter Doyo Jr.
Jacob Drake
Ab'm Dpuyster
James Drake
Susannah Drake
Mrs. Droyer
Anth. Duane
Antho. Duane
James Duane
Du Bois
Benjamin Dubois
Gerret Dubois
Hendrikus Dubois
Izack Dubois
Johanis Dubois
Lewis Dubois
Nathan Dubois
Samuel Dubois
Simon Dubois
Solomon Dubois
Hiskiea Du Boois
M. Dubourg
Johannis Duboys
William Duesenberry
Mary Duffie
Margaretta Duffield
Jacobus Dumon
Waldron Dumon
Cornelis Dumond
Rachal Dumond
Ragel Du Mont
Rachel Dunlap
William Dunlap
Edward Dunscomb
John Dupan
Dr. Duprey
Dr. Dupuy
Rich'd Durham
George Durje
Jakes Durje
Elias Durland Jr.
Elias Durlum
Elias Durlum ye 3d
Elias Durlun
Elias Durlun ye 3d
Jacob Durye
Daniel Duryea
Yost Duryea
Elizabeth Duryee
Benjamin Dusenbere
John Du Wint
Gerardus Duyckinck
Beniamin Dvsenbere
Samuel Dwight

Garrett Dyckman
Jacobus Dyckman
John Earl
Henry Eckford
Metcalf Eden
James Edmondstone
Philip Edsal
Richard Edsel
Richard Edsel Jr.
Geesje Een
Crestepher Eisenhart
Johannes Elderts
Ben. Eldridg
Ben Eldridge
Johannis Jury Elegh
Bastian Ellis
Samuel Ellis
Jno. Ellison
Mary Ellison
Thomas Ellison
William Ellison
Jno. Ellison Jr.
Jno. Ellison Sr.
John Ellison Sr.
Richard Elliott
Coenraat Elmendorp
Jakobus Elmendorph
Jenneke Elmendorph
Luycas Elmendorph
Petrus Ed Elmendorph
Cornelis Elmondorph
Jonathan Elmor
Ed Elsward
George Elsworth
Joris Elsworth
Margaret Elsworth
Theophil's Elsworth
Verdine Elsworth
William J. Elsworth
Jannoche Elting
Jakobus Eltinge
Jan Eltinge
Josiah Eltinge
Noah Eltinge
Andries Emans
Rebecca Emans
John Emauns
George Emigh
Corn's Euretse
Abrah. Evans
Jacob Evarston
Jacob Evartson
Robert Everdeen
M. Evers
Susan Evers
Ann Evits
Wm. Exon
James Fairlie
John Falconer
Benjamin Faneuil
Stn. Faniere

Benj. Fanneil
Benja. Fannil
Thomas Farmar
Jasper Farmer
Maria Farmer
Peter Fauconier
Theodore Fauconier
Peter Fauconnier
Johannes Feller
Hezekiah Ferguson
Mary Ferrari
Caleb Ferris
Edward Ferris
James Ferris
John Ferris
Matthys Fever
William Few
Anthony Field
Elizabeth Field
Nathan Field
Robert Field Sr.
Elizabeth Fine
Thomas M. Finlay
Philip Fiot
Ambros Fish
Nathaniel Fish
Samuel Fish Jr.
Samuel Fish Sr.
Harmanus Fisher
Leonard Fisher
Sam Fitch
Sam'l Fitch
Cornelius Flaman
Simon Fleet
Cornelus Fleman
John Flocker
Charles Floyd
Richard Floyd
William H. Folger
Folkert Folkertsen
Neclos Folkertsen
Jacob Fonseca
Charles Fonteyn
John P. Foot
Samuel Forbus
Benjamin Ford
Thomas Ford
Aron Forman
Charles Forster
John Fortuno
John Foster
Caleb Fowler
David A. Fowler
Elisabeth Fowler
Jeremiah Fowler
Theo. Fowler
Joseph Fox
Phebe Fox
Andr: Franccan

Glorianna Franklin
Henry Franklin
John Franklin
Thomas Franklin
Jacob Franks
Moses Franks
Tho. Franks
Myndert Frederickse
John C. Freeke
Hugo Freer
Isaac Freer
Widow Freers
Joseph Freland
Hendrick Freligh
Phil. French
Philip French
Phillip French
Andrew Freneau
Andrew Fresneau
Hannah Frost
Jacob Frost
Joseph Frost
Willm. Frost
Wright Frost
Capt. Fuller
Benjamin Funnel
Matthew Furber
Gabriel Furman
William Furman
Peter Gansevoort Jr.
Peter Gansevort
John Ganter
Francis Garabrant
Alexis Gardere
Nathaniel Gardiner
the Gardiner family
Thomas Garniss
Samuel Garritson
Ann Garting
John Gassner
James Gedney
Samuel Gedney
David Gelston
John Gelston
Maltby Gelston
Thomas Gelston
John Gen
Frances Gerbransen
James P. Germond
John Germond
Jacob Gesner
Nicholas Gesner
George Gibbs
Solomon D. Gibson
John Gidney
Nath. Gilbert
William W. Gilbert
Robert Gilchrist
Symen Gilde

Aquila Giles
Mr. Glaves
Johannes Glen
Sander Leendertsen Glen
John G. Glover
John J. Glover
Benja. Godfrey
Robert Ratson Goelet
Thomas Golding
Jacob Golst
Daniel Gomes
Mordica Gomes
Benjamin Gomez
Daniel Gomez
David Gomez
Isaac Gomez
Isaac M. Gomez
Jacob Gomez
Mord. Gomez
Mordecai Gomez
Mordica Gomez
Rebecca Gomez
Isaac Gomez Jr.
James Gordon
Stephen Gorham
Samwell Goslen
William Goslin
Isaac Gouverneur
Issac Gouverneur
Isaack Governeur
Nich's Governeur
Mr. Governous
Archibald Gracie
Chauncy Graham
Elizabeth Graham
Ennis Graham
Isaac Graham
James Graham
John Graham
Robert Graham
Thomas Greenall
Thomas Greenel
John Greenwood
Anna Grevenraedt
Nathan Gridley
Benjamin Griffen
Henry Griffen
Jonathan Griffen
William Griffen
Edward D. Griffin
Jonathan Griffin
Rob. Griffith
Rob't Griffith
William Griffith
John Grigg
John Griggs
John Grissman
Joseph Griswold
Johanis de Groet

Abraham Groot
John Grossbeek Jr.
John Guion
George Gunn
Hoysted Hacker
Bartholomew Hadden
Job Hadden
Thomas Hadden
Thomas Hading
Abraham Haesbrock
Abraham Haesbroeck, Jr.
Adrian Hagaman
Joseph Hagaman
Peter Hagaman
John Hagewout
Samuel Haight
Samuel Hake
Richard Hale
James Hall
Jno Hall
John and Ann Hall
Thomas Hall
the Hallet family
James Hallet
Joseph Hallet
Jacob Hallett
Richard Hallett
Robort Hallett
Samwell Hallett
Richard Hallett Jr.
Samwell Hallett Jr.
William Hallett Jr.
Samwell Hallett minor
Ezekiel Halsted
Philn. Halsted Jr.
Coenrad W. Ham
Alexander James Hamilton
Abijah Hammond
Charles Handasyde
Johannis Hardenberg
Abraham Hardenbergh
Leonard Hardenbergh
Abraham Hardenburgh
Gerardus Hardenburgh
Mr. Hardinbourg
John Haring
Samuel Haring
Mr. Harrison
Joseph Harriss
Ephraim Hart
James Hart
Peter G. Hart
Christian Hartel
Benjamin Hasbrouck
Daniel Hasbrouck
Isaac Hasbrouck
Isaack Hasbrouck
Jacob Hasbrouck
Sarah Hasbrouck

Isaac Hatch
Leffurt Haugewout
Elenor Haughwout
Widow Haughwout
Gabriel Havens
Henry Havens
Benjamin Haviland
Jon. Haviland
Joseph Haviland
Thomas Haviland
William Haviland
Sally B. Hawland
Thomas Hawsden
William Hawxhurst
Jacob Hay
David Hay Jr.
Benjamin Hay(e)s
David Hay(e)s
Michael Hay(e)s
Benjamin Haynes
Jane Haynes
Jos. Haynes
Benjamin Hays
David Hays
Judah Hays
Solomon Hays
Hendrick Heermans
Garrett Heermanse
Peter Heermanse
Adriaen Hegeman
Adrieaen Hegeman
Evert Hegeman
Rem Hegeman
Ann Helme
Arthur Helme
Catherine Helme
Jas. Henderson
Uriah Hendricks
Ari Hendrickse
Arl Hendrickse
Herry Hendrickse
Hendrick Hendricksen
Thomas Hendricksen
Delia Henry
Mr. Henry
James Hepburn
Andries Heremanse
Myer Hermance
Esther Heroy
Rennie Het
Rene Hett
Renne Hett
Rennie Hett
John Hewlet
Jown Hewlet
Daniel Hewlet Jr.
John Hewlet Jr.
Benjn. Hewlett
Danl. Hewlett
Henry Hewlett
Christopher Heysham

John Hibbard
Dennis Hicks
Edw'd & Aust'n Hicks
Jacob Hicks
Jacob M. Hicks
John Hicks
John M. Hicks
Oliver H. Hicks
Phebe Hicks
Samuel Hicks
Thomas Hicks
Jacob Hicks, Esq.
Jacob Hicks Jr.
Thomas Highan
Patrick G. Hildreth
Anthony Hill Jr.
John W. Hinton
Joseph Hitchcock
Miles Hitchcock
Stephen Hitchcock
John S. Hobart
Robert Hodge
Anthony Hoffman
Carl Hoffman
Elias Hoffman
Jacob Hoffman
Josiah Ogden Hoffman
Martin Hoffman
Martinus Hoffman
Nicholas Hoffman
Zacharias Hoffman
Adrian Hoghlandt
Cornelius Hogland
John Holdron
Edward Holland
David Holsted
Thomas Holsted
John Holt
John Hone
Philip Hone
Israel Honneywell Sr.
Israeli Honneywell Jr.
Israell Honneywell Jr.
Johnnathon Hont
Wilhelmus Hooghteling
Exors Adrian Hoogland
Harmanis Hooglant
Ann Hopper
James Hopson
Samuel Hopson
Sophia Hopson
George Hopson Jr.
Dirck Hornbeck
Israel and Timothy Horsfield
James Horton
Rev. Simon Horton
David Hosack
Israel Hosfield
Israel Hosfield Jr.
Joseph Houston Jr.
Joseph Houward

Mathew Howell
Goold Hoyt
James Hubbard
Robert Hudsen
Peter Huggeford
H. Hughes
George Hulit
Wager Hull
Andrew Hunt
Caleb Hunt
David Hunt
Jacob Hunt
Jo. Hunt
John Hunt
Obadiah Hunt
Stephanus Hunt
Stephen Hunt
Theodore Hunt
Thomas Hunt
Elijah Hunter
Gilbert Hunter
Governor Robert Hunter
John Huyler
Peter Huyler
Uriah Hyam
Charles Inglis
Madm. Ingoldshoes
Nathaniel J. Ingraham
John Ireland
Abraham Isaacs
Joshua Isaacs
Widow Ivers
Jno Jackson
John Jackson
Richard Jackson
Saml. Jackson
Thomas Jackson
Thomas F. Jackson
James Jackson Jr.
Benjamin Jacobs
Ralph Jacobs
Jehiel Jaggar
Loussique Francois Jaille
Elias Jamain
George James
Thomas James
R'd Janaway
George Janeway
Barent Jansen
Johannis Jansen
Thomas Jansen
Allan Jarret
Captain Jarret
Allan Jarrett
Anna Maria Jay
Aug't Jay
Augustus Jay
John Jay
Mary Jay
Mr. Jay
Nancy Jay

Peter Jay
Peter and Aug. Jay
Thos. Jefferys
Benijah Jervis
Thomas Jervis
Hendrick Johnsen
Annaca Johnson
Cort Johnson
Jeremiah Johnson
John Johnson
John B. Johnson
Teunis J. Johnson
William Johnson
Abra. Joneau
David Jones
Evan Jones
Gardner Jones
Humph'y Jones
Isaac Jones
James Jones
Rebecca Jones
William Jones
Thomas Jonson
Johannes Jonson Jr.
Benjamin S. Judah
Elizabeth Judah
Malgart Keater
Johannes Keater
John Keese
William Keese
Abraham Keip
Jack Keip
Roelof Keip
Gideon Kemberly
Elizabeth and Sarah Kemp
John Kemp
Robert Ken
William Kerby
Henry Kermit
Isaac Ketcham
Nathaniel Ketcham
Philip Ketcham
Solomon Ketcham
John Keteltas
William Ketteltas
Willem [or William] Kieft
Christofel Kiersted
Hans Kiersteden
Abraham King
Richard King
Rufus King
William King
Isabella Kingsley
James H. Kip
Samuel Kip
Benjamen Kipp
Peter Kipp
Walter Kippin
Thomas Kirbe
John Kirkland
Jacobus Kirstead

Daniel Kissam
Evert Knickerbacker
Harman Knickerbacker
Herman Knickerbacker
Calab Kniffin
David Kniffin
George Kniffin
George Knifin
Albert Koerton
Symon Kool
Cornelias Korsan
Catharine Kortright
Corn. Kortright
Jacob Kortright
John Kortright
Corn's Kortwright
Gerrit Kounover
Gerrit Kouwenhoven
Willem Kouwenhoven
Martin Kregier
Marten Krigier
John Laan
William Laight
Daniel Lake
Joseph Lake
John Lake Sr.
John Lamb
Johannes Lambert
William Lambert
Cornelis De Lametter
David De Lametter
Cornelis De Lametter Jr.
Margaret Lamourcun
Pamela Lamplin
Abram Landford
Metice Lane
Cornelis Langendyk
Lansing
Abr. Lansing
John Lansing Jr.
Jeremiah Lansingh
Willm. Larence
Jno. Larrance
John B. Lasher
Joseph Latham
Joseph Lattin
Judge Laurance
Sam'l Laurance
William Laurence
Arnaud Lavand
Henry Lawrance
Henry Lawrence
Jacob Lawrence
Jacobus Lawrence
John Lawrence
Jonathan Lawrence
Lawrence Lawrence
Thos. Lawrence
William Lawrence

Jesse Leatherwood
Nathan Leavenworth
Will Lecount
Wm. Lecount
Peter V. Ledyard
Abraham Lefever
Andrew Lefever
Mary Lefever
Nathaniel Lefever
Petronella Lefever
Jacobus Lefferse
Catherine Lefferts
Harmpje Lefferts
John Lefferts
Leffert Lefferts
Nicholas Lefferts
Peter Lefferts
William Legg
John Legg Jr.
Abraham Leggett
Abraham Lent
Jacobus Lent
John Leonard
Robt. Leonard
Robert LeRoy
Benjn. Lester
John Leverich
Joshua Levey
Moses Levey
Sam Levey
Pet'r Levingston
Philip Levingston
John Levirich
Arthur Levy
Eleazar Levy
Hayman Levy
Isaac Levy
Isaac H. Levy
Jacob Levy Jr.
Joshua Levy
M. Levy
Moses Levy
Sam Levy
Benja Lewes
Daniel Lewis
Francis Lewis
Fran's Lewis
Hannah Lewis
John Lewis
Macy Lewis
Nathaniell Lewis
Stephen Lewis
Zachariah Lewis
Abraham Liequare
John Liequare
Gatien Liger
Anthony Linch
Tho. Linch
William Lines

Elijah Lingo
Wid: Lininton
William Linn
Burger Lipkins
Amelia Lippincott
Anthony Lispenard
Livingston
Edward Livingston
Gilbert Livingston
Margaret Beekman Livingston
Peter and Phil. Livingston
Peter R. Livingston
Phil. Livingston
Philip Livingston
Phill. Livingston
Robert Livingston
Robt. Livingston Jr.
Phill Livingstone
Robt. Livingstone Jr.
Lloyd family
Henry Lloyd
Samuel Lockman
Ichabod Lontiit
Ichabod Lontitt
Govert Loockermans
Mary Jansen Loockermans
Lebbeus Loomis
James Loper
Daniel Lord
Joris Lot
Peter Lot
Abr'm Lott
Engelbart Lott
Englebort Lott
Hendrick Lott
Hendrick B. Lott
Isack Lott
Jacobus Lott
Johannis Lott
John Lott
Maurits Lott
Philip Lott
Johannes Lott Jr.
Abraham Louw
Henderica Louw
Petrus A. Louw
James Lovett
William Lovett
Cornel. Low
Is'c Low
John Low
John Lowerre
Frederick Lubbersen
Eldard Lucas
Charles Ludlam
Sarah Ludlam
Cary Ludlow
Gabriel W. Ludlow
Joseph Luis

William Lupton
Nicholas Luqueer
Rob. Lurting
John Lush
John Luyks
Abraham R. Luyster
Cornelius Lydacker
David Lydig
David Lyell
Anthony Lynch
Ma'r Lynch
Mary Lynch
Pet'r Lynch
Sa' Lynch
Thos. Lynch
Abr'm Lynsen
Joost Lynsen
Abr. Lynson
Dennis Lynt
Jacob Lynt
Peter B. Lynt
Andrew Lyon
Gilbert Lyon
Hannah Lyon
Joseph Lyon
Roger Lyon
Thomas Lyon
Wm. Lyon
Samuel MacCoune
Mr. Machado
John Machet
General Thomas Machlin
John MacKay
Alexander Macomb
Edw'd Man
Picard Manchel
Domyne Mansius
Francis Many
Cornelius Marcelius
Mrs. Marit
Isaac Rodrigues Marques
Christian Marschalk
P'r and Fr'cis Marschalk
Andrew Marschalk, Jr.
And. Marschalk Sr.
Andrew Marscollock Sr. & Jr.
Peter Marselis
Anthony Marshall
Mr. Marstan
Nath. Marstin
Jno. Marston
Nathaniel Marston
Thos. Marston
Nath. Marston Jr.
Barent Marteling
Roelof Martens
Adrian Martense
Adriaen Martense
Leffert Martense

Rem Martense
Alice Martin
Josiah Martin
Norris L. Martin
Robbard Marvil
John Mason
Johanis Masten
David Masterton
William Maxwell
Cornelius Maybe
Ann M'Adam
Charles McCarty
James McClogery
T. M'Collum
Daniel McCormick
Hugh McCormick
Widow M'Cullen
Charles McEvers
Malcom M'Ewen
Andrew McGown
M'Kinstry
David McKinstry
James McLeod
John McLeod
Charles Mecleen
Abraham Pereira Mendes
John Mercereau
Andrew Mercier
Joseph Merit
Charyty Merrill
Richard Merrill
Edward Merrit
John Merrit
Benjamin Merritt
John Merritt
Josuah Merseral
Peter Meserole
Ide Meyer
Moses Michal
Earsh Middagh
Garret Middagh
John Middagh
Christopher Mildeberger
Abraham Miller
Emma Miller
Mary Miller
Paul Miller
Silvanus Miller
Thomas Miller
James Milles
Isaac Mills
Jonas Mills
Jonathan Mills
Jonathon Mills
David Minsviele
Mangle Minthorne
Nathaniel G. Minturn
Mr. Minville
Jacob Misroll
John Misroll
Isaac Mitchell

Samuel Mitchell
Samuel L. Mitchell
John Mobrey
John Moffet
William Moleneor
John Monk
Baziled de Montaigne
John Montgomerie
John: Montonye
Allexander Moor
Jno. Moor
John Moor
Jon. Moor
Alex. Moore
Alexn Moore
Allex. Moore
Benjamin Moore
Boltis Moore
Jno. Moore
John Moore
John W. Moore
Joseph Moore
Judith Moore
Samuel Moore
Samuel Moore, Esq.
Samuel Moore, Lieut.
William Moore
Nathon More
Samwell More
Morel
Ben. Morgan
Caleb Morgan
Henry Morgan
Pet'r Morgat
Peter Morin
Pet'r Morine
Joseph Morrel
Andrew Morris
Gouverneur Morris
Lewis Morris
Richard Morris
Robert Morris
Robert Morris Jr.
Henry Mortison
Jacob Morton
Peter Moryne
Phebe Mot
Adam and Anne Mott
Henry Mott
Jacob Mott
James Mott
Patrick Mott
Valentine Mott
Motts
Adam Mount
Elesabeth Moures
Johannis Mourse
Samuel Mowris
William Moyles
Lewis Mulford
Rembt Folkern Muller

Hercules Mulligan
George Mumford
George Munro
Peter Jay Munro
George W. Murray
Andrew Myer
Christiyan Myer
Jacob Myer
Jacobus Myer
Peter Myer
William Myer
Myers
Adolph Myers
Emanuel Myers
John Myers
Judith H. Myers
Manuel Myers
Burger Myndertse
Myndert Myndertse
Jan Nagel
Phillip Nagel
Phillip Nagel Jr.
Mrs. Narett
Daniel Nash
Simon Nathan
Driek de Neack
Pierre George Negre
James Nevin
John Newel
Adriaen Newkerck
John Newkerk
Matthew Newkerk
Charles Newkirk [Nukerck]
Samuel Newman
William Niblo
Frances Nicolls
Wiliam Nicols
Lemountis Noe
Gerritt Noorstrant
Jan Noorstrant
Norton
George Norton
Robert B. Norton
Cornelia Norwood
Cornelia Van Clyff Norwood
Stephen Nottingham
William Nottingham
Joseph Nourse
Coenraat & Benyamen Nukerck
Cornelius Nukerck
Cornelius Nukerk Jr.
Charles Oakley
John Oakley
Alletty Oblenis
Bernard Oblenis
Albert Ogden
David A. Ogden
David B. Ogden
Euphemia Ogden
William Ogden
Thomas Ogilvie

Andrew Oliver
Hendrick Onderdonk
Henry Onderdonk
Elizabeth O'Neal
Tuenes Ooesterhout
Nelle Oosterhoudt
Elesabeth Oosterhout
William Oosterhout
Hendrick Oostrander
Magdalen Oothout
Francis Orrier
Michael Ortley
Samuel Osgood
Corneles Ostevanter
Stephen Ostrand
Rodriguo Pacheco
Rod. Pachego
Rodrigo Pachero
Joseph Paldon
Hendrick Palen
Catherine Palling
Benjaman Palmer
Ester Palmer
Lewis Palmer
Nehemiah Palmer
Phillip Palmer
Thomas Palmer
Wm. Palmer
Nehemiah Palmer Jr.
Adam Paorsen
David Pardo
Rodger Park
Roger Park Jr.
John Parker
William Parkinson
Pieter Parmetier
Thomas Parmyter
Thomas Parsall
John Parsel
Necolos Parsel
Thomas Parsell
James Parshall
Isrel Parshel
Levi Pawling
Catherine L. Payne
Sam'l Payton
Jacob Pearce
Caleb Pell
John Pell
Joshua Pell
Phebe Pell
Phebe Pell with Jos. Pell
Philip Pell
Stophell Pels
Richard Penfold
Hayes Pennell
Jacobus Persen
Matthew Persen
Harry Peters
Vall: Hewlet Peters
Joseph Petit Jr.

Charls Petors
John Petors
William Pettit
Alex. Phenix
James Phenix
Philip
Adolph Philipse
Mr. Philipse
Frederick Philipse
Adolph Phillips
George Phillips
Samuel Phillips
Phillipse
Adolph Phillipse
Alex. Phoenix
Allex Phoenix
Daniel Phoenix
Jacob Phoenix
Daniel Pie
Hezekiah B. Pierpont
Jeremiah Pierson
Neeltye Pietersen
Daniel Pine
James Pine
Wm. Pinfold
Isaac Pinheiro
Sam'l Pintard
Rachel Pinto
Adam Pitzer
Peter Pitzer
William Plaskett
Epenetos Plat
Vriah Plat
Epenetus Platt
Isaac Platt
Jonas Platt
Mary Platt
Sarah Platt
Zephaniah Platt
Zopher Platt
Barber Ploegh
Poulus Ploegh
Abraham Polhemus
Cornelius Polhemus
Daniel Polhemus
Garreta Polhemus
Jonathan Polhemus
The Rev. Mr. Polhemus
Theodorus Polhemus
Thomas Pollock
Henry Pope
Peter Porter
Garrit Post
Abrm. Post
Allison Post
Anthony Post
Jotham Post
William Post
Jotham Post Jr.

Apollos Potter
Cornelis Martensen Potter
George Potter
Gilbert Potter
Isaac Powell
John Powell
Martin Powles
Abraham Prall
Aron Prall
Ichabod Prall
Abraham Prevoost
John B. Prevost
Louis Prevost
Ebenezer Prime
Nathaniel Prime
Abraham Provoost
David Provoost
John Provoost
Wm. Provoost
Wm. T. Provoost
David Provoost Jr.
David Provost
Wm. Provost
John Pryor
John Pugsly
Elizabeth Pumroy
Caleb Purdy
Daniel Purdy
Henry Purdy
John Purdy
Joshua Purdy
Just Daniel Purdy
Roger Purdy
Isaac Pust
Tunis Quick
Arron Quinby
Christopher Radcliff
Jacob Radcliff
Jogham Raddely
John Rall
Jeromes Ramsen
Rem Ramsen
Jonathan Randell
John Randolph
Dina Rapalje
John Rapalje
Jeronemus Rapelie
Sara Rapelie
Haltje Rapelje
Abraham Rapelye
Cornelius Rapelye
Jacob Rapelye
Jeromes Rapelye
John Rapelye
Daniel Rapelye Jr.
Daniel Rapelye Sr.
Dina Raplje
Agnes Rappelyea
Mrs. Rattrat

Richard Ray
Jno. Read
John Read
Jos. Read
Catherine Reade
Jno. and Jo's Reade
Jos. and Jo'n Reade
Jacob Regnier
Mrs. Reid
Noble Reid
Peter Reid
Andros Reiker
Eliza F. Reilly
Jeremias Remse
Abram Remsen
Arsus Remsen
Derrick Remsen
Dirrick Remsen
Jeremiah Remsen
Jeremiah A. Remsen
Peter Remsen
Rem Remsen
Ja's Renaudet
Mr. Renehett
Marten Reyerse
Martin Reyerse
Mary Rhea
Barent Rhinders
Barrent Rhinders
Philip Rhinelander
Barrent Rhynders
Jon. Richard
Paul Richard
Paul Richards
William Richardson
Wm. Rickets
Joseph Ridgeway
Cornelius Rierson
Georg Rierson
Caleb S. Riggs
Benjamin Right
Denis Right
Joseph Rigway
Abraham Riker
Anna E. Riker
John L. Riker
Richard Riker
Isaac Riley
Mr. Rindell
George Risoer
James Rivington
Sarah T. Roach
John Roads
Christopher Robart
Jeremiah Robbins
John Robbins
Willet Robbins
Th: Robert
Nicholas Roberts

Eliza Robins
Jos. Robinson
Thomas Robinson
Nathaniel Rochester
Rebeckah Rockwell
Samuell Rodman
Azel Roe
Henry Roe
William Roe
David Rogers
Henry Rogers
Thomas Rogers
Zopher Rogers
Joseph Rolf
Jno. Roll
John Roll
John Roll Jr.
Jno. Rolland
John Rolland
Jon. Rolland
John B. Romeyn
Nethanel Roo
John Rooke
Lawrence Roome
William Roome
John Roon
Abraham Roosa
Albert Roosa
James J. Roosevelt
Mr. Roosevelt
Nicholas Roosevelt
Peter Roosevelt
William Root
Henry Rose
John Roseveldt
Jacob Rosevelt
Jno. Rosevelt
Jon. Rosevelt
Nicholas Rosevelt
C. Rousseau
Henry Row
John Rowland
Samuel Rowland
Sarah Rowll
Joseph Royall
Maria Magdalen Ruble
Jasper Ruckle
Silas Rushmore
Thomas Rushmore
Anth. Rutgers
Anth'n and Peter Rutgers
Henry Rutgers
Aleda Rutsen
Anthony Ruttgers
Jan Ryerse
Jacob Ryerson
Leffert Ryerson
John Ryerson Jr.
Bernard Rylander

Barr't Ryndert
Lewis Sack
Joseph Sacket
Joseph Sackett
William Sackett
Lawrence Salisbury
Catharine Salter
John Samis
Nehemiah Sammis
Abram Sandford
Cornel. Sandford
Comfort Sands
James Sands
Joshua Sands
Lewis Sands
Simon Sands
Abraham Santvoord
Capt. Sarly
Jacob Sarly
Abraham Sarzedas
William Saxton
Thomas Sayrs
Gideon Schaats
Reynier Schaats
John Schank
Rier Schemerhorn
Symon Schemerhorn
Abraham Schenck
John Schenck
Marten M. Schenck
Steve Schenck
Martin Schenck Jr.
Abraham Schenk
Arnot Schermerhorn
Arnout Schermerhorn
John Schermerhorn
John S. Schermerhorn
Simon Schermerhorn
Symon Schermerhorn
Peter Schermerhorne
Cornelius Schoonmaker
Frederick Schoonmaker
Hannah Schoonmaker
Hendrick Schoonmaker
Tedotia Schoonmaker
Cornelius Schoonmaker Jr.
Herculus Schureman
the Schuyler bros.
the Schuylers: Aaron, Adoniah,
 John, and Peter
Aaron Schuyler
Arent Schuyler
Cornelia Schuyler
John Schuyler
Peter Schuyler
Pet'r and Adoniah Schyler
Joseph Scidmore
John B. Scott
Bridget Scudder
Moses Scudder
Pompey Scudder

Timothy Scudder
Samwell Scuder
Philip Scuyler
Maria Seabury
The Rev. Mr. Seabury
David Seaman
Edmund Seaman
Isaac Seaman
Jacob Seaman
James Seaman
Jonathan Seaman
Obediah Seaman
Robert Seaman
Samuel Seaman
Thomas Seaman
William Seaman
Zebulun Seaman
Thos. Seaman Jr.
Adam Seamans
Soln. Seamanß
Sarah Seamons
Thomas Seamons
Daniel Searing
Jacob Searing
John Searing
Samuel Searing
James Searle
John Searle
Cornel Sebring
Isaac Sebring
Chris: Seehar
Chrispr. Seehar
Stephen Sell
William Sell
Anthony Semans
John Semicon
Francis Seney
James Seton
Wm. H. Seward
William Sexton
Drake Seymour
Florenta Seymour
Thomas Seymour
Wm. Seymour
Wm. Seymour Sr.
Ezekel Shadbolt
John Shannon
Ann Sharp
Peter Sharpe
Charles Shaw
John R. Shaw
Susan Angenes Sheeferen
Giles Shelley
David Shepeord
Dirck Shepmoes
Ruth Sheppard
Ruth Shepperd
Moses Sherwood
Catherine Shoemaker
Joseph S. Shotwell
John S. Sickles

William Sickles
Dow Sidam
Jacob Siemon
Louis Simmond
William Simmones
Margret Simonson
Simon Simonson
Nath. Simpson
Solomon Simpson
Nathan Simson
Nat'l Simson
Sampson Simson
Tunus Skank
Simeon Skillin
Abraham Skillman
Beniamin Skillman
Abraham Skilman
Benjaman Skilman
Thomas Skinner
Anthonia Slachboom
Antonia Slachboom
John Slegh
Abraham Sleght
Hendrick Sleght
Hendrickus Sleght
Matthew Sleght
John Slidell
Isaac Sloat
Nathan Smades
Aldert Smedes
Benjamen Smedes
Petrus Smedus
Alexander Smith
Andrew Smith
Ann Smith
Benjamin Smith
Caleb Smith
Cornell Smith
Daniel Smith
Edmund Smith
Epenetus Smith
Faulintine Smith
Floyd Smith
Henry Smith
Isaac Smith
Jacob Smith
James Smith
Jeams Smith
Jno Smith
Job Smith
John Smith
John B. Smith
Joseph Smith
Josiah Smith
Josias Smith
Lemuel Smith
Nancy Smith
Nathaniel Smith
Obadiah Smith
Otheniel Smith
Philetus Smith

Phinehas Smith
Richard Smith
Sarah Smith
Solomon Smith
Stephen Smith
Thomas Smith
Timothy Smith
William Smith
Daniel Smith Jr.
James Smith Jr.
Obadiah Smith Jr.
Obadiah Smith Sr.
Bull Smiths
Isaac Snediker
Jacob Snediker
John Sneyden
Rachel Sniffin
Marta Snyder
Haym M. Solomon
Sim. Souman
Robert Speir
Philip Spencer
Henry Spingler
Geertye Splinter
Abraham Springsteen
David Sprong
Hastings Stackhouse
Thomas Stagg
Amelia Staples
John Staples
David Stebbins
Cornelis Steenwyck
Bengaman Steimets
Rulef Stephens
Enoch Stephenson
John Stevanson
Ebenezer Stevens
John Stevens
Cornelius Stevenson
Edward Stevenson
Enoch Stevenson
Hector St. John de Crevecoeur
Nicholas Stickel
Nicholas Stillwell
Richard Stillwell
Samuel Stilwell
Sarah Stilwell
Richard Smith Stonebrook
Wilhelmus Stoothof
Wilhelmus Stoothof Jr.
Garnet Storm
Garrit Storm
Jacob Storm
Thomas Storm
Peter Stots
Jacob Stout
Jeremiah Stout
John Stoutenburgh
Thomas Stoutenburgh
Daniel Strang
John Striker

Selah Strong
Cornelious Stryker
John Stryker
Peter Stryker
Andris Stucholm
Andrew Stuckey
Joseph Studwell
Strong Sturges
Nicholas William Stuyvesant
Peter Stuyvesant
William Stymets
Jon. Suar'l
Hendrik Sudam
Lammert Sudam
John Suffern
Jon. Sutcliffe
Richard Suthard
Joseph Sutton
Samuel C. Sutton
Evert Suydam
Hendrick Suydam
John Suydam
Eva Suylandt
James Swan
Powlas Swart
Barnadus Swarthout
John Swartwout
Jan Sweerts
Joseph G. Swift
James Swords
Nathaniel Sylvester
Sarah Taber
Silas Talbot
Samuel Talman
Jan Tamassem
Benjamin Tanbroeck
Coenradt Tan Broeck
John Tanbroeck
Pieter Tappen
Tjatie Tappen
John Taylor
Richard Taylor
William Taylor
Isaac Teller
Johannes Teller
William Teller
John T. Tenbrock
Petrus Ten Brock
Blandiena Tenbroeck
John C. TenBroeck
John Ten Broock
Daniel Ten Eyck
Tobias Ten Eyck
Jenneke Ten Eyk
Roeliff Terhunen
Joseph Sacket Tert:
Arie Terwillegen
Petrus Tesschenmaeker
Ebenezer Theale

Hannah Theale
Thos. Theall
Abreham Theat
Christiana Theobald
Jno. Theobalds Jr.
Charles Thield
Joseph Thield
De Prune Thilorier
Justin Thilorier
Mich. Thody
Johanis Chris Thomas
John Thomas
Lane Thomas
Mary Thomas
Samuel Thomas
John Thomas Jr.
Jan Thomassen
James Thompson
Samuel Thompson
William Thompson
Jeame Thompsone
Tho. Thong
Thos. and Rip Thong
Walter Thong
Dan'l Thorn
James Thorne
Richard V. W. Thorne
John Tibout
John Tickell
Andrew Tid
Teunis Tiebout
Henry Tiel
Lauwrence Tiel
Thomas Tillotson
James Tillott
Edward Titus
Elisabath Titus
Elizabeth Titus
Francis Titus
Jacob Titus
Mary Titus
Michael M. Titus
Peter Titus
Richard Titus
Sarah Titus
Stephan Titus
Stephen Titus
Walter Titus
Widow Titus
William Titus
Margaret Todd
Pamela Todd
George Toevelt
George Adam Toevelt
Tompkins
Daniel Tooker
John Tooker
Nicholas Toorn
Peter Toten

John Tounsend
Daniel Tourneur
George Towers
Joseph Towers
John Townsand
Richard Townsand
Anne Townsend
George Townsend
Henry Townsend
James Townsend
John Townsend
Meribah Townsend
Micajah Townsend
Nathaniel Townsend
Phebe Townsend
Richard Townsend
Samuel Townsend
Silvenus Townsend
Timothy Townsend
William Traphage
Mary Tredwell
Samuel Tredwell
Thomas Stars Tredwell
Thos. Tredwell
Antoni Trip
Johannes Troumbour
Robert Troup
James Tucker
Thomas Tucker
Tho. Tudor
Jakop Turck
George Turnball
Phebey Turner
Benjamin Tusten
James Tuthill
Solomon Tuthill
Eleazer Tyng, Esq.
Philip Udle
Thomas S. Uffington
Abraham Underhill
Amos Underhill
Anthony L. Underhill
Daniel Underhill
Nathaniel Underhill
Samll. Underhill
Thomas Underhill
Joseph Vail [or Veal]
Thomas Vail
Peter Valet
Peter Valete
Cronimus Valkenburgh
Obediah Vallentine
Thomas Vallentine
Thomas Vallentine Jr.
Mr. Vallet
Peter Vallet
Peter Vallett
Peter Vallette
Abraham J. van Alstine

Philip van Alstine
Simon Van Antwerp
Barrent Van Benthouse
John Van Benthouse
Gerrit Van Benthuysen
John Van Benthuysen
Beekman Van Beuren
Doctor V: beuren
John Van Beuren
Sylvester Van Beuren
John Van Blarcom
Claes Jansen van Bockhoven
Cornelius Van Borsum
Henry V'n borssom
Henry V'n Borssom
Jno. Vanbrough
Captain Vanbrugh
Adriance Van Brunt
Cornelius Vanbrunt
Litgert Van Brunt
Roelof Van Brunt
Rutgert Van Brunt
Wilhelmis Van Brunt
Rutgert Van Brunt Junior
Rutgut Van Bruunt
Elsye Van Bunschoten
Van Buren
Capt. Johan Vanburgh
Captain Van Burgh
Lawr'ce Vanbuskirk
Jacob Van Cortland
Van Cortlandt
Jacobus Van Cortlandt
Oloff Stevens Van Cortlandt
Fred V. Cortlant
David Van Cots
Fred Van Courtland
Fred Vancourtland
Jacob van Curlear
Rich'd Vandam
Rip van Dam
Rip Van Dam
Rip Van Dam Esq.
Barent V: Defenter
Mr. Vandham
Annetje van de Merken
John C. Vandenheuvel
Anna Vanderbilt
Helena Vanderbilt
Jeremiah Vanderbilt
Jeremyes V: D: bilt
John V. Der Bilt
Rem V: D: bilt
Seytje V: D Bilt
Vanderburgh
Jacob D. van der Heyden
Cornelis V D Hoef
Jno. Vanderhule
John Vanderhule

Peter Cornelius Vander Veen
Cornelis Van D: Veer
Jeromus V: D: Veer
John V: Der Veer
Pieter V D Voort
Abraham Vandewater
John Vandike
Mrs. Vandike
Barent Jansen van Ditmars
Van Doune
Mr. Van Doune
Mr. Vandrieson
Jan Vanduese
Cornelis V: Duyn
Gerrit Van Duyn
Abraham Van Duzer
Thomas Van Dyck
Jan van Eps
Jacobes Van Ette
Jacobes Van Ette, yr.
Haert Van Foerhees
Heart Van Foerhees
Cathlynje Van Fretenborg
Abrm. Van Gaasbeck
Lawrence Van Gaasbeck
Thomas Van Gaasbeck
John Van Gaasbeek
Wyn'ts Vangant
Evert Van Gelder
Phoebe Van Gelder
Abrah. Vanghorn
Abr. Vanhorn
Corn. Van Horn
Cornelius Vanhorn
Dav. V'n horn
Gar't Vanhorn
Garret Vanhorn
Garrett Vanhorn
Gerrd Vanhorn
Jno. Vanhorn
John Vanhorn
Mr. Vanhorn
Abraham Vanhorn Jr.
Corn's Vanhorn Jr.
Corn's Vanhorn Sr.
Van Horne
Abr. Vanhorne
Abraham Van Horne
Abraham Vanhorne
Abram Vanhorne
Augustus V. Van Horne
Corn. Vanhorne
Cornelius Van Horne
Cornelius Vanhorne
Garret Van Horne
Garret Vanhorne
Garrit Vanhorne
Garr'tt Vanhorne
Gerr't V'n Horne
James Van Horne
Jno. Vanhorne

John Van Horne
John Vanhorne
Abraham Van Horne Jr.
Abraham Vanhorne Jr.
Guybert Van In Burgh
Gysbert Vaninburgh
Abraham Van Keuren
Benjamin Van Keuren
Jacobus Van Keuren
Tryntje Van Keuren
Peter Van Luven
Gilbert Van Mater
Charles G. Van Megen
George Vannolst
John Van Nostrand
Winche Van Nostrand
Joost Vannuis
Jacobus Van Nuys
Willem Van Nuys
Willem Van Nuys Jr.
Jon. Vanpelt
Jon. Vanpelt Sr.
Peter Van Pelt
Petrus Van Pelt
Wouten Van Pelt
Claes van Petten
Claes Fredericksen van Petten
Cornelius V. Van Ranst
Cornelius W. Van Ranst
Jeremaias van Rensselaer
Peter Van Rensselaer [also
    spelled Van Renssellaer and
    Van Rensselaer]
Philip Van Rensselaer
Jeremiah Van Riper
Richard Van Riper
Cornelius van Ruysen
Wyn't Vansant
Van Schaaks
Wessel Van Schack
Philip Van Schaick
Johannes V: Sickelen
Farnandus Van Sicklen
Fernandus van Sicklen
Ryman Van Sigelen
Dominie Van Sindere
Aderian C. Van Slyck
Rachel Van Steenbergen
Aaras Van Steenbergh
Minard Vansyckley
Peter Vantilborough
Andrew Van Tuyl
Otto Van Tuyl
Wouter Van Twiller
Clos Vanvaughty
Van Vechten
Sweer Teunissen van Velsen
Barent Van Vleck
Roelif Van Voorhees
Zacharia Van Voorhis
Zacharias Van Voorhis

Johannes Vanwaganan
Solomon Vanwaganan
Evert Van Waganen
Garret van Waganen
Johen Van Waganen
Lea Van Waganen
Gerrit Van Wagene
Johannis Van Wagene
Abraham Van Wagenen
Art Van Wagenen
Garret van Wagenen
Gerret Van Wagenen
Jacob Aarts Van Wagenen
Cornelius S. Van Winkle
Peter Van Wit
Van Wyck
Hendrick Van Wyen
Van Zandt
John Van Zandt
Peter Van Zandt
Wynant Van Zandt
Godardys Van Zolingan
Isaac Varian
Abraham Varick
Jacobus Varick
John Varick
Richard Varick
Domyny Vas
Jas. Vaughan
Jasen Vaughan
Jason Vaughn
Philip Vdle
John Vegte
Philip Veller
John Veltmon
Thomas Vendemerk
Thomas Venkeuran
Antje Ver Kerck
Gul. Verplank
Gul'n Verplank
Johnston Verplank
Johannes Verveleen
Arnout Carnelissen Viele
Cornelis Viele
Philip Vielle
Phillip Vielle
Benjamin Vincent
Francis Vincent
Sam'l Vincent
Jacob Vinross
Mathew Visscher
John Voahears
Nathan Volentine
Jacob Volingtine
Ephraim Vollingtine
Jacob Vollintine
Jonathan Vollintine
Madame Jeanne Mathusine
    Droibillan Volunbrun
Joseph Vondel
Neeltye Voorhears

Abraham Voorhees
Adriaen Voorhees
Cornelis Voorhees
Cornelius Voorhees
Amadoor Vopie
John Vosburgh
Adam Vrooman
Hendrick Vrooman
James D. Wadsworth
Benjamin Waldron
Jno. Waldron
John Waldron
Samuel Waldron
Jon Waldron Sr.
Benjamin Walker
Richard L. Walker
John Walter
Jno. Walter
Jon. Walter
Jno. Walters
Walton
Corn. Walton
Gerard Walton
Jacob Walton
Thomas Walton
William Walton
Wm. Walton Jr.
Wm. Walton Sr.
Christian Wanamaker
Bartholomew Ward
Jasper Ward
Mary Warden
Thom. Ware
Willett Warne
Abigail P. Warner
George Warner
John Warring
Benjamin Waters
John Waters
Robert Waters
Samuel Waters
Elizabeth Watkins
James Watson
John Watt
Jo. Watter
Antony Watters
John Watts
Jeams Way
Samwell Way
Anth'y Web
Samuel Webb
George Weekes
Able Weeks
William Weeller
Addem Weesner
Hennery Weesner
Thomas Welling
Obadiah Wells
Barent Wemp
Myndert Wemp
Abraham Wendell

Abram Wendell
Mary Wenham
Hugh Wentworth
Rout Wessels
Agnes West
William West
Apollos Wetmore
James Wetmore
Eliphalet Wheeler
Sebastian Wheeler
John White
Daniel Whitehead
Fred J. Whiting
Stephen Whitney
Henry Whitson
Elesabeth Whittak
Daniel Whittaker
Edward Whittaker
Hillitie Whittaker
John Whittaker
John Wick
Azariah Wickes
Justice Eliphilet Wickes
Philip Wickes
Israel Wickham
Parker Wickham
Elnathan Wicks
Vullard Widbeck
William Wilcocks
Richard Wilis
John Wilkes

Jacob Wilkins
Marshall R. Wilkins
Amos Willes
Capt. Willet
Isaac Willet
Thomas Willet
Richard Willets
Colonel Willett
Elisha Williams
Jemimah Williams
John Williams
Jonas Williams
Mary Magdalen Williams
Nathll. Williams
Richard Williams
Robert Williams
William Williams
Steven Williamse
Nicholas Williamsen
Peter Williamson
Anna Willis
Rebeckah Willis
Richard Willis
Samuel Willis
William Willis
John Willis Jr.
Ralph Williston
William Willit
Richard Willits
Isaac Willitt
Thomas Willitt

Abraham Wilson
Elisabeth Ann Wilson
John Wilson
Joseph Wilson
Peter Wilson
Samuell Wilson
Martin Wiltse
David Windfield
Joseph B. Windsor
Levinus Winne
Peter Winne
Joseph L. Winter
Dirck Pieterson Wittepaert
Jakoba Wittiker
John Woatman
Marritje Woertman
Pieter Woglum
Benjamin Wolsey
Benjamin Wolsey Jr.
Hanah Woo
Israel Wood
John Wood
Joseph Wood
Priscilla Wood
William Wood
Joseph Woodard
Anthony Woodhouse
Selah S. Woodhull
Calvin Woodruff
Asel Woodworth
Melanchthon Lloyd Woolsey

Melanthon Taylor Woolsey
Tunis Wortman
George Wray
Grove Wright
Isaac Wright
Jacob Wright
Jordan Wright
Sarah Wright
Zuroiah Wright
Daniel Wurts
Henry J. Wyckoff
Peter Wyckoff
Cornelis Wykhoff
Gerrit Wykof
Johannis W. Wykof
Pieter Wykof
Luykas Joh. Wyngaard
Antie Wynkoop
Derck Wynkoop
Evert Wynkoop
Johannis Wynkoop
Tobias Wynkoop
Yate
Daniel Youngs
George Youngs
John Youngs
Thomas Youngs
Harmon Yurcksea
Alexander Zuntz

Selected Bibliography

Afro-Americans in New York Life and History, vols. 1-22 (Jan. 1977-Jan. 1998).

Alexander, Arthur J. "Federal Officeholders in New York State as Slaveholders, 1789-1805." *Journal of Negro History* 28, no. 3 (July 1943).

Caro, Robert A. *The Power Broker: Robert Moses and the Fall of New York.* New York: Alfred A. Knopf, 1974.

Catterall, Helen T., ed. *Judicial Cases Concerning American Slavery and the Negro*. Vol. 4, *Cases from the Courts of New England, the Middle States, and the District of Columbia*. Washington, DC: Carnegie Institution of Washington, 1936.

The Colonial Laws of New York from the Year 1664 to the Revolution. Vols. 1 & 2. Albany, 1894.

Davis, Thomas J. "New York's Long Black Line: A Note on the Growing Slave Population, 1626-1790." *Afro-Americans in New York Life and History* 2, no. 1 (January 1978): 41-59.

Davis, Thomas J. *A Rumor of Revolt: The "Great Negro Plot" in Colonial New York*. New York: Free Press, 1985.

Davis, Thomas J. "'These Enemies of Their Own Household': A Note on the Troublesome Slave Population in Eighteenth-Century New York City." *Journal of the Afro-American Historical and Genealogical Society* 5 (1984): 133-47.

Deyle, Steven. "'By farr the most profitable trade': Slave Trading in British Colonial North America." *Slavery and Abolition* 10, no. 2 (September 1989): 107-25.

Donnan, Elizabeth, ed. *Documents Illustrative of the History of the Slave Trade to America*. Vol. 3, *New England and Middle Colonies*. Washington, DC: Carnegie Institution of Washington, 1932.

Ellis, David M., et. al. *A Short History of New York State*. Ithaca, NY: Cornell University Press in cooperation with the New York State Historical Association, 1957. Revised, 1967.

Farley, Ena L. "The Denial of Black Equality Under the States Rights Dictum: New York, 1865-1873." *Afro-Americans in New York Life and History* (January 1977).

Foner, Philip S. *Business & Slavery: The New York Merchants & the Irrepressible Conflict*. New York: Russell & Russell, 1968.

Fox, Dixon Ryan. "The Negro Vote in Old New York." *Political Science Quarterly* 32 (June 1917): 231-262.

Gardner, Robert Wallace. "A Frustrated Minority: The Negro and New York City Politics of the 1880s as Typified by the Mayoralty Election of 1886." *The Negro History Bulletin* 29, no. 4 (January 1966).

Gilje, Paul A. *The Road to Mobocracy: Popular Disorder in New York City, 1763-1834*. Chapel Hill, NC: University of North Carolina Press, 1987.

Goodfriend, Joyce D. *Before the Melting Pot: Society and Culture in Colonial New York City, 1664-1730*. Princeton, NJ: Princeton University Press, 1992.

Goodfriend, Joyce D. "Burghers and Blacks: The Evolution of a Slave Society at New Amsterdam." *New York History* 59 (April 1978): 125-44.

Goodheart, Lawrence B. "'The Chronicles of Kidnapping in New York': Resistance to the Fugitive Slave Law, 1834-1835." *Afro-Americans in New York Life and History* 8, no. 1 (January 1984): 7-15.

Graymont, Barbara. "New York State Indian Policy After the Revolution." *New York History* 57 (October 1976): 438-74.

Headley, Joel T. *The Great Riots of New York, 1712 to 1873.* New York, 1873.

Hirsch, Leo H., Jr. "The Negro and New York, 1783-1865." *Journal of Negro History* 16, no. 4 (October 1931).

Hodges, Graham Russell, and Alan Edward Brown, eds. *"Pretends to be Free": Runaway Slave Advertisements from Colonial and Revolutionary New York and New Jersey.* 1994.

Horsmanden, Daniel. *The New York Conspiracy.* Boston: Beacon Press, 1971.

Ireland, Ralph R. "Slavery on Long Island: A Study of Economic Motivation." *Journal of Long Island History* 6, no. 1 (winter 1966): 1-12.

Janvier, Thomas A. "New York Slave-Traders." *Harper's New Monthly Magazine*, January 1895.

Johnson, James Weldon. *Black Manhattan.* New York: Atheneum, 1930. Reprint, 1968.

Kappler, Charles J., comp. *Indian Affairs: Laws and Treaties.* Vol. 2. Washington, DC: U.S.G.P.O., 1904.

Kerber, Linda K. "Abolitionists and Amalgamators: The New York City Race Riots of 1834. *New York History* 48, no. 1 (January 1967): 28-39.

Korbin, David. *The Black Minority in Early New York.* New York: University of the State of New York, 1963.

Lader, Lawrence. "New York's Bloodiest Week." *American Heritage* 10, no. 4 (June 1959).

Launitz-Schurer, Leopold S., Jr. "Slave Resistance in Colonial New York: An Interpretation of Daniel Horsmanden's New York Conspiracy." *Phylon* 41, no. 2 (June 1980): 137-52.

Lindsay, Arnett G. "The Economic Condition of the Negroes of New York Prior to 1861." *Journal of Negro History* 6, no. 2 (April 1921): pp. 190-99.

Lydon, James G. "New York and the Slave Trade, 1700 to 1774." *William and Mary Quarterly*, 3d ser., 35, no. 2 (April 1978): 375-94.

McKay, Ernest A. *The Civil War and New York City.* Syracuse, New York: Syracuse University Press, 1990.

McManus, Edgar J. *Black Bondage in the North.* Syracuse, NY: Syracuse University Press, 1973.

McManus, Edgar J. *A History of Negro Slavery in New York.* Syracuse, NY: University of Syracuse Press, 1966.

Morgan, Edwin Vernon. "Slavery in New York, with Special Reference to New York City." In *Slavery in the States: Selected Essays.* New York: Negro Universities Press, 1969.

Moss, Richard Shannon. *Slavery on Long Island: A Study in Local Institutional and Early African-American Communal Life.* 1993.

Nammack, Georgiana C. *Fraud, Politics, and the Dispossession of the Indians: The Iroquois Land Frontier in the Colonial Period.* Norman, OK: University of Oklahoma Press, 1969.

Nordstrom, Carl. "The New York Slave Code." *Afro-Americans in New York Life and History* 4, no. 1 (January 1980): 7-25.

Northrup, A. Judd. "Slavery in New York: A Historical Sketch." *New York State Library Bulletin*, History No. 4 (May 1900).

O' Callaghan, E. B. *The Documentary History of the State of New-York.* 4 vols. Albany, 1849-51.

O'Callaghan, E. B., and Berthold Fernow, eds. *Documents Relative to the Colonial History of the State of New York.* 15 vols. Albany, 1853-1887.

Olson, Edwin. "The Slave Code in Colonial New York." *Journal of Negro History* 29, no. 2 (April 1944): 147-65.

Ottley, Roi, and William J. Weatherby, eds. *The Negro in New York: An Informal Social History.* With a preface by James Baldwin. New York: New York Public Library; Dobbs Ferry, NY: Oceana Publications, 1967.

Porter, Kenneth W. "Relations Between Negroes and Indians Within the Present Limits of the United States." *Journal of Negro History* 17, no. 1 (January 1932).

Ratner, Lorman. *Powder Keg: Northern Opposition to the Antislavery Movement, 1831-1840.* New York: Basic Books, 1968.

Riddell, William Renwick. "The Slave in Early New York." *Journal of Negro History* 13, no. 1 (January 1928): 53-89.

Roff, Kenneth L. "Brooklyn's Reaction to Black Suffrage in 1860." *Afro-Americans in New York Life and History* 2, no. 1 (January 1978).

Rury, John L. "The New York African Free School, 1827-1836: Conflict Over Community Control of Black Education." *Phylon* 44, no. 3 (1983).

Scott, Kenneth. "The Slave Insurrection in New York in 1712." *The New York Historical Society Quarterly* 45, no. 1 (January 1961): 43-74.

Skinner, Don C. "New Evidence of Black Unrest in Colonial Brooklyn." *Long Island History* 12 (fall 1975).

Stuart, William. "Negro Slavery in New Jersey and New York." *Americana* 16 (1922): 347-64.

Szasz, Ferenc M. "The New York Slave Revolt of 1741: A Re-Examination." *New York History* 48, no. 3 (July 1967): pp. 215-30.

Trelease, Allen W. *Indian Affairs in Colonial New York: The Seventeenth Century.* Ithaca, New York: Cornell University Press, 1960.

Wagman, Morton. "Corporate Slavery in New Netherland." *Journal of Negro History* 65, no. 1 (winter 1980).

Wallace, Anthony F. C. *Death and Rebirth of the Seneca.* New York: Alfred A. Knopf, 1970.

Weyl, Nathaniel, and William Marina. *American Statesmen on Slavery and the Negro.* New Rochelle: Arlington House, 1971.

Wiecek, William M. "The Statutory Law of Slavery and Race in the Thirteen Mainland Colonies of British America." *William and Mary Quarterly*, 3d ser., 34 (1977): 258-80.

Index

THE RECLAMATION PROJECT
Hidden History Series

Massachusetts, "The Cradle of Liberty," was the first to officially welcome the African slave trade! It was the leading slave ship builder and among the leaders of the annihilation of the Red man and woman. All this and much more in a revealing new booklet. Easy-to-read, fully footnoted, fascinating info. By Tingba Apidta; 64 pages - $5.95 / ISBN - 1-892705-01-X

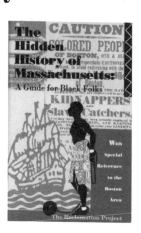

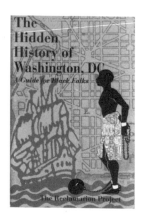

Washington, DC was known as **The Congo of America**! Find out about the Black History of: The *Pocahontas* Story • D.C. Slave Laws • Washington Monument • Jefferson & Lincoln Memorials • White House Slavery • African slaves who built the Capitol • **Includes a map of SLAVE SALE SITES in Washington, DC**, and much, much more!! By Tingba Apidta; 80 pages - $8.95 ISBN - 1-892705-02-8

Support Your Local Black Bookstores